ENCOUNTERING DEATH
Structured Activities for Death Awareness

IRA DAVID WELCH, Ed.D.
Professor, Counseling Psychology
University of Northern Colorado
Greeley, Colorado

RICHARD F. ZAWISTOSKI, M.Div.
Lutheran Campus Pastor
Indiana University
Bloomington, Indiana

DAVID W. SMART, Ph.D.
Director, University Counseling Center
University of Northern Colorado
Greeley, Colorado

ACCELERATED DEVELOPMENT INC.
Publishers
Muncie   Indiana

ENCOUNTERING DEATH:
STRUCTURED ACTIVITIES FOR DEATH AWARENESS

1 2 3 4 5 6 7 8 9 10

Printed in the United States of America

Technical Development: Tanya Dalton
                         Marguerite Mader
                         Sheila Sheward

Cover Design: Dennis Hill

Library of Congress Cataloging-in-Publication Data

Welch, I. David (Ira David), 1940-
    Encountering death : structured activities for death awareness /
Ira David Welch, Richard F. Zawistoski, David W. Smart.
         p.   cm.
    Includes bibliographical references and index.
    ISBN 1-55959-021-1 (pbk.)
    1. Death--Social aspects--United States.   2. Death--United States-
-Psychological aspects.   I. Zawistoski, Richard F., 1947-   .
II. Smart, David., 1939-   .   III. Title.
HQ1073.5.U6W45   1991
306.9--dc20   91-70336
                                            CIP

LCN: 91-70336

ISBN: 1-55959-021-1

Order additional copies from

ACCELERATED DEVELOPMENT Inc., Publishers
3400 Kilgore Avenue, Muncie, Indiana 47304-4896
(317) 284-7511
Toll Free Order Number 1-800-222-1166

DEDICATIONS

"To my wife, Marie, and our sons, David and Dan, who help me create an appreciative awareness of life."

I. David Welch

"To my wife, Patsy, and children, Ann and Carl, for the variety of life lived and shared."

Richard F. Zawistoski

"To my wife, Julie, and my children, John, Margaret, Elizabeth and Mary, for their constant love, help, and support."

David W. Smart

ACKNOWLEDGMENTS

The authors wish to thank *Time, Inc.* for permission to publish a graphic that heightens awareness of the impact of guns on violent death in America. We also wish to thank the Rose Medical Center, Robert Wood Johnson Foundation, Poudre Valley Hospital Foundation and St. Joseph Hospital for permission to use information gained in a survey entitled, "Colorado Speaks Out On Health." Finally, we extend our appreciation to Dr. Joe Hollis for his careful and helpful editing of the original manuscript.

The Authors

PREFACE

Each of the authors teaches classes in death and dying. Two of us are psychologists and the third is a minister. We came to an understanding of the need for classes in death and dying from our educational backgrounds, our personal histories, and our interactions with others coping with death and dying in their lives.

As we reflect on our experiences, two sorts of impressions stand out in our minds. First, people were grieving about the loss of someone they loved and at the same time were worrying if they were "grieving in the right way." Next, those who in one way or another could be characterized as denying the pain of the loss they had suffered are the ones who might act callously or indifferently or respond intellectually about the death. Through these observations, we came to the conviction that classes in which people learned about death and dying could do much to help all of us live more effectively.

Any class in death and dying includes what might be called the academics of death. These include important information on the statistics of death, numbers of people who attempt suicide and complete suicide, the cultural influences which affect our attitudes toward death, and economics of death. We are more tolerant and more understanding when we know about stages of death and dying and tasks of mourning. Textbooks for death and dying classes are informative and helpful in our understanding of the topic of death and dying.

Why, then, write a book such as this in which the class, as a group and as individual class members, examines, in a more personal way, many of the topics of death and dying? Quite simply, because as teachers of these courses, we have repeatedly seen how understandings from shared personal experience and from reported individual experience have equal importance with the academic information in death and dying classes. Again and again, in many different ways, we found our students telling us that the experiential exercises and personal sharing components of our classes were the ones that were most meaningful. These activities were often seen as "thought provoking," "moving," and "catalytic," and often seemed to increase motivation to read and understand the academic, fact-oriented parts of our courses. Some students made clear and direct statements of preference for such experiential activities while others gave more indirect indications of such preferences. Examples of such indirect communications included increased attendance and more active participation in class. Occasions when the students as a groups, or as individuals, have been able to interact with one another and tell each other their stories, to report their growth-enhancing and growth-diminishing experiences have been the classes that have had the greatest impact and most lasting effect on students.

For these reasons we have tried to put together many activities that involve the class members in a more personal and in-depth understanding of death and dying. We have tried to provide in-class activities that provoke class members to examine their personal and cultural attitudes and assumptions about death.

We invite students to examine their beliefs to see if their current "truths" result in the compassion, commitment, and caring they want to demonstrate to those they love. Do beliefs they presently hold represent a death denying orientation toward life, or do they result in practices that demonstrate the compassion and care they would want and expect from people who care about them? If after such an examination they find their values are one's that they wish to maintain, then they can hold them with conviction. They have been examined and found worthwhile.

The intent of this book is not to replace standard textbooks on death and dying. It is meant to be used as a supplement to the texts which provide the academic information necessary to any real understanding and examination of societal assumptions and attitudes toward death and dying. This book presents a number of stimulating and provocative activities that will help class members confront death and dying in a more personal and lasting manner.

One aspect of this book's usefulness is in its adaptability and flexibility. The activities may be used in part or in whole. They may be done sequentially or at random. They may be used in a variety of settings including programs for nurses, clergy, counselors, and other professionals as well as in general undergraduate collegiate courses in death and dying. While the reader may choose to use the activities in any order desired, they have been ordered in a particular sequence. Chapter 1, "Encountering Death in the Self," was chosen as the first chapter so as to build the foundation of increased self-awareness for the study of death and dying. In addition, a need to personally encounter death seemed to be a strong motive for many of the students who enrolled in our courses and our intention was to meet these needs by addressing the students' personal expectations, experiences, feelings, and knowledge early in the course.

Chapter 2, "Encountering Death in the Family," appeared to be a natural progression after Chapter 1 since, for most, the early and enduring relationships of the family are particularly relevant to death encounters. We recognize that in recent years American families have taken new and different forms including step families, blended families, and single parent families. We have, accordingly, provided activities which are appropriate for a wide variety of family circumstances. In these cases, the adaptability and flexibility of format may be particularly helpful.

Chapter 3, "Encountering Death in the Culture," is intended to help students become more perceptive about cultural influences upon their attitudes toward death. Our experience as teachers has convinced us of the strength, yet subtlety, of cultural influences upon us. The activities outlined in Chapter 3 deal with such topics as media, language, music, humor, and ethnic customs, and were chosen to give students insight into these cultural influences.

Chapter 4, "Encountering Death in Our Institutions," Recognizes that society has moved from one based upon agricultural to one more urbanized and with more centralized power in government or corporate structures, therefore institutions representing these structures have had greater and greater influence upon us. The image of death presented to us by institutions thus has an important influence upon us.

Chapter 5, "Encountering Unexpected Death," is designed to help students explore deaths which ordinarily lie outside their control. Death is, in many ways, always unexpected. The deaths caused by murder, accidents, and disasters are difficult to understand. They defy the control we have gained over so many other aspects of our lives. The activities in this chapter are aimed at a discussion of the fear, impact, and peculiar difficulties of coping with this form of death.

Chapter 6, "Encountering Death in Suicide," responds to a topic which has received an increasing amount of media attention in recent years, primarily due to the increase in youth suicide. Suicide is high on the list of causes of death yet often remains obscure and misunderstood because it is such a frightening and guilt-producing form of death. The activities included in this section are designed to counter the denial of suicidal death, increase our understanding of its prevalence, expose its myths, and provide strategies for prevention.

Chapter 7, "Encountering Death in AIDS," provides activities aimed at exploring this epidemic killer. Recently, AIDS has commanded our attention. It has affected a great many people both directly and indirectly. It has challenged the way we approach relationships. It has drawn some people closer while building barriers for others. Students need help so as to move beyond the knowledge and prevention mode into the arena of emotions and meanings. Activities in this chapter are designed to encourage the sharing of personal feelings, thoughts, and fears about the various issues with AIDS. In doing so the hope is that all can dare to take another step toward understanding and acceptance of AIDS—victims, families, and friends.

Chapter 8, "Encountering Death in Our Values," provides an arena in which students can experience the push and pull of various ethical dilemmas as they struggle to resolve many of the complicated issues which face us in this frontier of medical and technological knowledge. Likewise, explorations in spiritual and religious values are provided in this chapter.

Chapter 9, "Encountering Death as a Helper," provides an opportunity to explore a variety of topics which arise in the helping process. Issues are presented in ways that make these topics real, immediate, and practical. These activities are designed to help students understand that one need not be a professional in order to be of help to others.

Thus, all of these chapters will bring an immediacy and an experiential dimension to the understanding of death and dying which will stimulate students to a more meaningful encounter with death. Our sincere belief and hopefully that of students who use this book is that increased ability to cope effectively with death will help us to lead more effective lives.

PRE-TEST
ENCOUNTERING DEATH SCALE

Purpose: To determine the degree to which one sees one's own ability to cope with death.

Time: 10 Minutes

Activity Procedure:

1. Respond to each question on the 5 point scale from "strongly agree" to "strongly disagree."

2. Respond to the "Encountering Death Scale."

3. When all members of the group have completed the "Encountering Death Scale", sum the class response to each question and divide by the number of responses to each item so as to determine the class average for each item.

ENCOUNTERING DEATH SCALE

Directions: Please indicate your response to each of the statements using the following scale:

Strongly Disagree	Disagree	Neutral	Agree	Strongly Agree
1	2	3	4	5

_____ 1. I am at ease in thinking about death.

_____ 2. It is important to discuss death and death related topics.

_____ 3. I am prepared to face my own death.

_____ 4. I can be helpful in assisting others to face death.

_____ 5. I can help someone who is feeling suicidal.

_____ 6. I can talk about death with others.

_____ 7. I understand the role of many of society's institutions (hospital, church, funeral home, nursing home, etc.) in dealing with death.

_____ 8. Sudden death is very frightening to me.

_____ 9. I understand my fears about death.

_____ 10. I understand my culture's response to death.

_____ 11. I can talk with a dying person.

_____ 12. I can share my thoughts and feelings about death with family members.

_____ 13. I understand how AIDS is transmitted.

_____ 14. I can assess the seriousness of a suicide threat.

_____ 15. I can help others who have faced death in a natural disaster.

_____ 16. I can help someone deal with the death of a pet.

_____ 17. I can assist others who are grieving a death.

_____ 18. I understand the ethical problems that accompany prolonged terminal illnesses.

_____ 19. I can plan a funeral.

_____ 20. I can help my family members deal with death.

Discussion and Reflection:

1. When you looked at the class summary, how did you compare? _____
_____
_____

2. In what areas did you more strongly agree? _____
_____
_____

3. Write what you believe may account for your strong agreements. _____
_____
_____

4. In what areas did you more strongly disagree? _____

_____

_____

5. Write what you believe may account for your strong disagreements. _____

_____

_____

6. Review your responses and identify those areas where you feel you need to have better skills in coping with death. Those areas are

_____

_____

_____

CHAPTER 1

ENCOUNTERING DEATH IN THE SELF

1. SELF

Any understanding of death and dying must begin with ourselves. Whatever actions we take begin with our own understandings. For the authors, the self represents a construct, a way of understanding human action. For us the Self is an understanding of who we are. It is what we mean when we say "I" or "Me." Because of that understanding we see all experience as filtered through the self. For that reason, the reader can understand why encountering death in the self is such an important aspect of any class in death and dying. Beyond the academics, of course, is the personal concern of every person with living a life which is meaningful and effective for him/her. Our belief is that one way life becomes more meaningful and effective is by coming to an understanding of death and, to one degree or another, making peace with it. Therefore a rational, sensible, and right way to begin the search for peace with death is to begin with the self.

Each of us holds fears, doubts, and questions about death. This is not an uncomfortable assertion to make. What is more difficult for many of us is that the fears and doubts, left unchallenged, end up directing our behavior. The fears come to rule our behavior. Perhaps, this is nowhere more important than in our relationships. The peculiar relationships that surround death and dying can be profoundly affected by the fears, doubts, and questions each of us has about death. If we are so fearful of our own death, then reaching out to others when they are dying can be extremely difficult. Many of us fear death and, yet, overcome that fear by an act of courage to talk and comfort someone who is facing death. Others of us do not. For those of us who do not, the people we love might die alone and without the companionship and comfort because of fearful family or friends. Thus, what becomes clear is that encountering one's own fears can have a direct effect on relationships. The difference may be between being or not being physically present and emotionally available for one's parents, one's siblings, one's spouse, one's children. Overcoming our fear of death may mean being the kind of friend who can be of comfort rather than a representative of a death denying culture which retreats into silence and absence. That is the importance of encountering death in the self as it relates to others.

Another reason for encountering death in the self is to live a more effective life. Some may see the desire to live a more effective life as a selfish desire. And, we suppose that could occur and would be a negative aspect. Still, we need to recognize that we cannot be of much service to others if we do not take care of ourselves. We believe many people in this world will strive to make peace with themselves who need not be construed as selfishness. We recommend an attitude of wholesome concern with the self in which one aspect of that concern is encountering death in the self. The outcome of a successful encounter with an understanding of one's own death is the ability

to plan the future;

to make a will;

to make decisions about the disposition of one's body;

to make decision about organ donation;

to provide for the future of one's spouse and children;

to reflect upon the values by which one actually wishes to live one's life; and

other concerns of life that come to mind only after one faces the fears, doubts, and questions of death.

The challenge of this chapter is to encounter death in the self. In spite of what some have said, one can look death in the eye and gain from the experience. You can encounter your fears and doubts and by doing so live a more effective life. That is the invitation of this chapter.

Activity 1.1
EXPECTATIONS

Purpose: To explore goals and objectives of this class.

Time: 30 minutes

Activity Procedure:

1. Answer the following questions individually. Write your responses in the space provided.

   a. Why did you take this class? _____

   _____

   _____

   b. What do you hope to learn from this course? _____

   _____

   _____

   c. What fears or expectations do you have? _____

   _____

   _____

   d. How willing are you to be involved in this class on a personal level? _____

   _____

   _____

2. In small groups, share your answers.

3. Have someone summarize the discussion of your small group for the entire class.

Discussion and Reflection:

1. After meeting in the small groups and hearing others expectations, reflect upon your answers, and note on answers to Items 1.a. through 1.d. any changes you might make.

2. How were your responses similar to others in the class? _____

   _____

   _____

3. How were your responses different from others in the class? _____

   _____

   _____

4. What goals and objectives came as a surprise to you? _____

   _____

   _____

Activity 1.2
PERSONAL DEFINITIONS

Purpose: To realize that definitions of death may affect our behavior.

Time: 20 minutes

Activity Procedure:

1. Complete the following chart by writing a definition for each of the three terms.

2. Write when you believe each of the states occur.

State	Definition	When
Death:		
Dying:		
Dead:		

Discussion and Reflection:

1. What differences do you see in your definitions? _____

_____

_____

2. Which infer life; which infer no life?

life: _____

no life: _____

3. In what order do these events occur? _____

_____

_____

4. How is it that our definitions determine how we respond to people who are dying or grieving?

_____

_____

_____

5. What difference is there, if any, in the definitions of "living" and "dying"? _____

_____

_____

Activity 1.3
FACING DEATH

Purpose: To identify one's own fears about death.

Time: 15 minutes

Activity Procedure:

Using the scale below, rate each of the following areas regarding the degree of fear for you.

1 = minimal   2 = slight   3 = mild   4 = moderate   5 = severe

A. _____ death in general   H. _____ murder

B. _____ your own death   I. _____ suicide

C. _____ parent(s)   J. _____ disasters

D. _____ grandparent(s)   K. _____ cancer

E. _____ spouse   L. _____ heart attack

F. _____ child(ren)   M. _____ accidents

G. _____ pet   N. _____ friends

Discussion and Reflection:

1. How did this activity heighten, if it did, the awareness of your fears? _____
   _____
   _____

2. Does your answer to Number 1 surprise you? Why or why not? _____
   _____
   _____

3. What did you learn by doing this activity? _____
   _____
   _____

4. What is the next step for you in dealing with your fears? _____
   _____
   _____

Activity 1.4
FEARS OF DEATH

Purpose: To become aware of the commonly held fears of death.

Time: 15 minutes

Activity Procedure:

1. Appoint a class member to be a recorder of responses on the chalkboard.

2. Begin with any student or the instructor and continue until each class member has responded to the questions: "When I think about death or dying, what I fear is . . ." If any class member says nothing, then the stem would be "If I had a fear about death or dying, it would be . . ."

3. Have the recorder write, in as brief a form as possible, each response.

4. When all class members have responded, using the list of "Nine Common Fears of Death and Dying," match, if possible, class members' responses with specific items of the nine.

    The Nine Common Fears of Death and Dying* are as follows :

    a. What happens after death

        (1) Fate of the physical body (corruption, decay)
        (2) Judgment (punishment, after death life review)
        (3) Unknown (nothingness, no life after death)

    b. Fear of the process of dying

        (4) Pain (long painful, drawn out illness, violence)
        (5) Indignity (circumstances of embarrassment, disfigurement)
        (6) Burden (financial, long-term care)

    c. Loss of life in general

        (7) Loss of mastery and control (decisions, rationality)
        (8) Incompleteness (issues in life, children not grown)
        (9) Separation from life (leave everything and everyone we have ever known and loved)

Discussion and Reflection:

1. How closely did Neale's common fears match the fears of the class members? _____

_____

_____

_____

*List developed by Robert E. Neale, Union Theological Seminary

2. What, if any, fears were listed by class members that were not listed by Neale? _____

_____

_____

3. Given that so many of our fears are "common," how does this fit with the idea that death is highly personal and individual? _____

_____

_____

Activity 1.6
ATTITUDE INVENTORY

Purpose: To assess personal attitudes toward death and dying.

Time: 15 minutes

Activity Procedure:

1. Across the chart below are various and widening societal categories. Down the left hand column are death related stimulus words. Fill in the chart with a word or two that reflects your perception of how each category of society feels about the corresponding death related words.

2. Then gather in small groups and share your answers.

ATTITUDES TOWARD	SELF	FAMILY	CLASSMATES	INSTI-TUTIONS	CULTURE
Example funerals	unsure	traditional	don't know	profit making	denial
FUNERALS					
DYING					
MURDER					
ACCIDENTS					
DISASTERS					
SUICIDES					
AIDS					
GRIEF COUNSELORS					

Discussion and Reflection:

1. What pattern of words seemed to repeat itself? _____
   _____
   _____

2. What questions about perceptions do you most want to ask your classmates? _____
   _____
   _____

3. In comparing your responses to your classmates, what differences did you note? _____
   _____
   _____

4. Compared to others in your group, how accurate do you consider your responses
   to be? _____
   _____
   _____

Activity 1.7
IMPACT OF DEATH

Purpose: To examine feelings about the impact of death.

Time: 20 minutes

Activity Procedure:

1. Looking back upon your death experiences, reflect upon the following continua and circle the number which reflects where you feel you are.

		1	2	3	4	5	
a.	strengthened	1	2	3	4	5	weakened
b.	enhanced	1	2	3	4	5	diminished
c.	self-confidence	1	2	3	4	5	insecurity
d.	strengthened faith	1	2	3	4	5	loss of faith
e.	learned much	1	2	3	4	5	learned little
f.	acceptance	1	2	3	4	5	denial

2. Working as a group, make a class summary chart. (Numbers have been used to assist you in your tabulations)

Discussion and Reflection:

1. What did the summary chart tell you about the general feelings of the class? _____
   _____
   _____

2. Is the summary in keeping with society and tradition?

   _____ Yes   _____ No

3. If different, what might help explain those differences? _____
   _____
   _____

4. If differences do exist, how can we reconcile these differences? _____
   _____
   _____

Activity 1.8
DEATH PREFERENCES

Purpose: To enhance awareness of death preferences.

Time: 20 minutes

Activity Procedure:

1. Place an X at the appropriate place on each of the continuums. Even though we may not have control over the manner in which we die, we may have preferences how our life ends. How do you prefer to die?

		1	2	3	4	5	
a.	violent						quiet
b.	old						young
c.	expected						unexpected
d.	with people						alone
e.	ordinary						heroic
f.	sudden						lingering

2. Working as a group, make a class summary chart.

Discussion and Reflection:

1. On which continua, if any, were you much different from the class summary? _____
   _____
   _____

2. As you reflect on these differences, what might help explain those differences? _____
   _____
   _____

3. What conflicts or contradictions, if any, existed between your answers? _____
   _____
   _____

4. Reflect upon your reactions to these conflicts or differences and write what those reflections are. _____
   _____
   _____

5. Would you sacrifice your life for another?   _____ Yes   _____ No

6. Under what circumstances? _____
   _____

Activity 1.10
RISK-TAKING BEHAVIORS

Purpose: To assess your risk-taking behaviors, and determine their level of risk.

Time: 15 minutes

Activity Procedure:

1. List what you think are risk-taking behaviors in each of the following categories. (An example is given for each.)

SEX	EATING	TRANSPORTATION
unprotected sex	bingeing	no seat belts
_____	_____	_____
_____	_____	_____
_____	_____	_____

WORK	HOME	DRUG/ALCOHOL
hazardous materials	frayed extension cord	more than 2 drinks a day
_____	_____	_____
_____	_____	_____
_____	_____	_____

2. Review your responses in Item 1 and as you do score your risk-taking inventory according to the following scale by writing a number in front of each behavior you listed.

   never = 0   once = 1   occasionally = 3   frequently = 5

3. Sum the scores for each category and calculate your average score for each category:

   _____ sex   _____ eating   _____ transportation

   _____ work   _____ home   _____ alcohol/drugs

Category Rating:

   0 = low risk   1 to 2 = mild risk
   3 to 4 = moderate   5 and above = high risk

Total Scoring: Eliminate all "frequent = 5" scores and then sum the categories to arrive at a total score.

   Overall Rating: _____

4. Add all scores in Item 3 and divide by number of categories scored to obtain an average risk score which for you is _____.

Discussion and Reflection:

1. To what extend do you agree with what your total score reflects? _____
   _____
   _____

2. If you answered "often" for any of the activities, how do you rationalize your behavior? _____
   _____
   _____

3. Are any friends of yours engaged in high-risk behavior? What can and do you say to them? _____
   _____
   _____

4. What would need to occur to make you change any high-risk behaviors? _____
   _____
   _____

5. Have any of these listed behaviors resulted in close calls with death for you? _____ Yes _____ No

6. For a friend? _____ Yes _____ No

7. If yes to either or both Items 5 and/or 6, has this precipitated any change in you? _____
   _____
   _____

8. Why do you think you and/or other people engage in these behaviors? _____
   _____
   _____

9. How do you differentiate between risk-taking which is necessary and stimulating to life and that which is merely foolish? _____
   _____
   _____

Activity 1.11
PLAN YOUR OWN FUNERAL

Purpose: To think about planning a personal funeral service.

Time: 40 minutes

Activity Procedure:

In this exercise you will begin to plan in detail your own funeral service. What would happen? What music would be played and/or sung? By whom? Who would be there? What readings would you include?

Begin with the questions below. Elaborate as it becomes necessary for you.

1. Identify the kind of service.

    a. What would be its theme? _____

       _____

       _____

    b. Who would participate and what would they do and say?

Name	Comments	Role
(1) _____	_____	_____
(2) _____	_____	_____
(3) _____	_____	_____
(4) _____	_____	_____
(5) _____	_____	_____
(6) _____	_____	_____
(7) _____	_____	_____
(8) _____	_____	_____
(9) _____	_____	_____

2. Identify the music if any.

    a. What music would you want to be sure was included? Why? If no music, explain why.

       _____

       _____

       _____

b. Write out some of the lyrics that would be especially meaningful. _____

_____

_____

_____

3. Identify the readings, if any, that are given to the service.

a. What readings (poetry, prose) would you want to be heard by the people attending?

_____

_____

_____

b. Include some of them here. _____

_____

_____

c. What special meaning do you want conveyed during this service? _____

_____

_____

_____

4. Identify the order of the service. What would be done first? A processional? Music? Then what?

_____

_____

_____

5. Identify the location of the service. Where would all of this take place?

_____

_____

_____

6. Now, write your own eulogy. What do you want people to remember about you? Remember this will be read aloud to the people present at your service. _____

_____

_____

_____

_____

_____

_____

_____

_____

7. Write your own epitaph. _____

_____

_____

_____

_____

_____

_____

_____

Discussion and Reflection:

1. As you prepared your funeral service, of what thoughts and feelings were you aware?

_____

_____

_____

2. What feelings emerged regarding your family (mother, father, spouse, children, brothers, sisters)?

_____

_____

_____

3. Did you find one section more difficult to complete than another? If so, which one?

_____

_____

_____

4. Reflect on why the section identified in the last question was more difficult.

_____

_____

_____

CHAPTER 2

ENCOUNTERING DEATH IN THE FAMILY

2. FAMILY

Most of us are born into a family. In the modern world, families come in a bewildering number of forms. Yet, whatever form our family takes it becomes the crucible out of which we emerge as persons. Our values, our life choices, our selection of mates, our professions all are deeply influenced by the family into which we are born and live. No topic, outside ourselves, seems to be more important than the family when considering death and dying.

Our first experiences with death are frequently with a family member—one of our grandparents, sisters, brothers, parents or the family pet. The response of our family to death is where our values first begin to form regarding death and dying. Is death something to be feared? Is death a question that can be raised in our family? Will our fears be laughed at? Will lies be told in order not to face death squarely and directly? In the answer to these questions, and others, we have the beginnings of how each of us learned about death and dying.

To understand our early memories is to reflect upon the past. To recount the past is necessary sometimes in order to have an understanding of where our present values and assumptions originated. To encounter one's past may be necessary in order to dispel some area of ignorance. One can look at the past without having to condemn it. The way we learned, the way we were taught, or the attitudes and assumptions of our childhood do not have to be condemned. The world has changed and what once was has changed. This is nowhere more true than in the attitudes of childrearing and family values. While children were once considered to be too fragile to be told about important family matters such as money problems, sex, family squabbles, and death, today more families believe that involvement of children in all aspects of family life is very important. The willingness to talk about death and dying in the family is a major shift in attitude in modern American society. Children of today have grown up with a more open attitude to a number of sensitive parts of living. This is true about death and dying. It is no longer as unthinkable to talk about funeral arrangements with aging parents, with dying siblings, or even with a close friend. The family begins our understanding of death and dying. Our relationship with our family does not exist in the past. It exists in the present. We need to encounter death and dying in our families in the present. The older one grows, the more likely he or she is to have to face death. To encounter death in the family means to face the reality that our loved ones will someday die. The attitude of the past has been that this idea is too painful to face and should not be talked about. The inclusion of death and dying as one more area of life which can be openly talked about holds a promise: that the sometimes isolated, lonely and frightening death of family members is of the past.

The future is not here. It is being designed right now. What family values do each of us wish to teach for the future regarding death and dying? Is it necessary that the death practices of the past and the present be the death practices of the future? What changes need to be made? Encountering death in the family becomes important as one more way to insure that our fears, doubts, and questions do not result in relationships in which our love and compassion are not expressed.

Activity 2.1
PARENTAL LOSS

Purpose: To confront one's feelings about the death of a parent.

Material: Pen and pencil or two different color writing instruments.

Time: 10 minutes

Activity Procedure:

1. On the line graph, chart the impact of the death of your mother in each of the areas listed. If your mother has died, do this as you remember the impact. If your mother has not died, do this as you anticipate the impact. Use "M" for mother.

2. On the line graph, chart the impact of the death of your father. Use "F" for father.

3. Use two colors (e.g. red for mother and black for father) and connect the points to make line graphs.

High Impact

Low Impact   economic   emotional   social   spiritual   nurture   school

father (pen color) _____   mother (pen color) _____

Discussion and Reflection:

1. What differences did you observe between parents? _____

_____

2. Compare with those in class who have experienced the death of a parent with those who have not. What are the differences? _____

_____

_____

Activity 2.2
YOUR HOMETOWN

Purpose: To identify places of death during your life.

Time: 20 minutes

Activity Procedure:

1. Draw a map of your hometown, community, neighborhood. or area.

2. Find and mark on your map the following places:

   a. cemetery or cemeteries
   b. funeral home(s)
   c. where deaths have occurred that you remember, i.e., accidents, home, school, church, hospital, and other significant places.

Discussion and Reflection:

1. What feelings did these places hold for you? (fear, awe, sacred etc.)

   _____

   _____

   _____

2. Were you surprized at the feelings some of the places elicited from you?

   _____

   _____

   _____

3. Did you or any of your friends change your behavior around any of these places?

   _____

   _____

   _____

Activity 2.3
THE SHOCK WAVES OF DEATH

Purpose: To realize the ripple effect a death has on us.

Material: Pen and pencil or two different color writing instruments.

Time: 20 minutes

Activity Procedure:

1. Add to the following list any significant others in your life. Use a letter to designate the person.

   M—mother (step-mother)   U— uncles
   F—father (step-father)   GF—grandfather
   B—brothers   GM—grandmother
   Si—sisters   C—cousins
   A—aunts

2. First place your name in the center, then from the list above, place members of your family and significant others in your life on the graphic, a "Shock Wave of Death," so as to indicate your shock at their deaths or how shocked you would be at their deaths. Place those of greatest shock nearer the center.

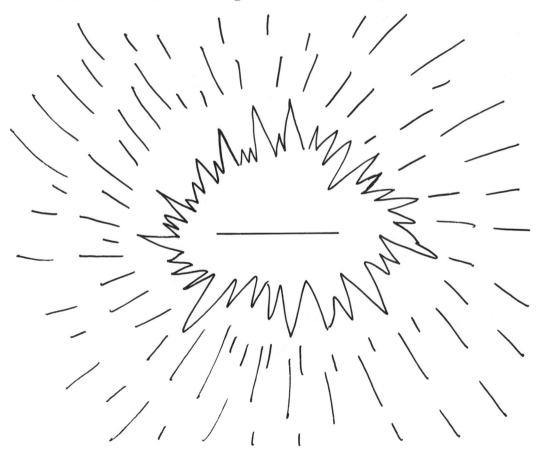

3. Now place the following kinds of people in the same "explosion" above. Use a different color pen or pencil to add the letters representing these people.

E—entertainer   Pu—US politician
N—neighbor   Pw—World politician
T—teacher   R—minister, rabbi, etc
St—stranger

Discussion and Reflection:

1. Did different deaths fall in different places in the explosion? Were you surprised at any of them?

_____

_____

_____

2. Did a public figure have more impact than a family member? Why?

_____

_____

_____

3. What determines the intensity of a death for you? For others? (geography, relationship . . .)

_____

_____

_____

Activity 2.5
CHILDHOOD UNDERSTANDINGS

Purpose: To recall, reflect, and compare your childhood understandings with those gathered from research.

Time: 20 minutes

Activity Procedure:

1. Write a narrative, or use key words that describe how you remember feeling or think you may have felt about death at each of the ages below.

How I Understood Death	
At present:	
age 15:	
age 10:	
age 5:	
age 3:	

2. Compare what you and others in your group have written with the findings of researcher Maria Nagy:

Stage I:	3—5 years old (post-toddler, preschool)	Death is temporary, a continuation of life; being asleep; neither universal nor personal.
Stage II:	5—9 years old (elementary school)	Death is final; personified; neither universal nor personal; death can be eluded.
Stage III:	9—up (Jr. Hi and up)	Death is final, personal and universal.

3. Compare them with the works of J. Piaget and D. Elkind.

Stage 1:	3—5 yrs.	Don't understand death and do not see it as discontinuous with life.
Stage 2:	6—9 yrs.	Discontinuous with life but reversible and not applicable with everyone.
Stage 3:	10-11 yrs.	Death is irreversible and seen as a medical/biological/scientific event.

PREOPERATIONAL: Anthropomorphic—Believes that many physical objects are alive. They have feelings, intentions and purposes. Past and future are barely grasped and the present looms large. Children at this stage may say that death is like, "you go to sleep" or that the dead are "hungry" as reflected in some change of state but nonetheless as continuous with life.

CONCRETE: Pragmatic—While death is the end of life, it is the beginning of another. While it happens to some people, it doesn't happen to everybody. The concrete operational child shows a number of contradictions about death.

FORMAL: Scientific—Accepts death as a fact of nature and know that they will die and that the people they love will die as well.

Discussion and Reflection:

1. How did your memories compare with the theorists?

_____

_____

_____

2. What might account for the differences?

_____

_____

_____

3. Did you like one theory better than another? Why?

_____

_____

_____

Activity 2.6
CHILDHOOD FRIENDS WHO DIED

Purpose: To realize the effect of the death of a peer.

Time: 10 minutes

Activity Procedure:

1. Chart how many deaths you remember of your peers and how they died. You may use marks, or write their names.

	Natural	**Accidental**	**Suicide**	**Homicide**
Elementary				
Jr. High				
Sr. High				

Discussion and Reflection:

1. How do you remember these affecting you? Do one or two stand out? Share the story with the group. How is it still affecting you?

_____

_____

_____

2. How did you grieve the death? Is it finished?

_____

_____

_____

3. After comparing the charts of the whole class, make summarizing statements. Are there any patterns? Where do the highest numbers fall? Why?

_____

_____

_____

Activity 2.7
CHILDHOOD GAMES, SONGS AND RHYMES

Purpose: To recall references to death in leisure and play.

Time: 40 minutes

Activity Procedure:

1. Make as complete a list as possible of the following childhood activities that relate to death. Use common references as well as an original one you remember. (Ring around the Rosie; cops and robbers; fairy tales; etc)

Nursery Rhymes	Songs	Games	Toys

2. In small groups

   a. Share a nursery rhyme or two,
   b. Share a song or two,
   c. Play one of the games, and
   d. Tell about your toys.

Discussion and Reflection:

1. How do you remember the effect of these songs, games and toys on your childhood?

   _____

   _____

   _____

2. Were there differences between male and female games, toys, songs, rhymes?

   _____

   _____

   _____

3. As you reflect upon it now, how have childhood games, toys, etc. influenced your attitudes toward death?

_____

_____

_____

Activity 2.8
BROTHERS AND SISTERS

Purpose: To explore the trauma of the death of a sibling on oneself and the family system.

Time: 20 minutes

Activity Procedure:

1. Order the following list of feelings as you experienced them or would probably experience them at the death of a sibling.

depression	relief	shame	embarrassment
loneliness	sorrow	fear	resentment
guilt	anger	glad	responsibility

#1. _____   #5. _____   #9. _____

#2. _____   #6. _____   #10. _____

#3. _____   #7. _____   #11. _____

#4. _____   #8. _____   #12. _____

2. Explain your ordering in the small group.

3. Compare answers with those who have experienced the death of a sibling.

Discussion and Reflection:

1. How much of you died (would die) at the death of a sibling?

_____

_____

_____

2. How much of your family died or would die?

_____

_____

_____

3. What role(s) was lost in the family with the death?

_____

_____

_____

4. If some class members have suffered the death of a sibling, are their listings different from those who have not? How?

_____

_____

_____

_____

Activity 2.9
PETS: ARE YOU PREPARED?

Purpose: To affirm grief feelings at the death of a significant pet.

Time: 15 minutes

Activity Procedure:

Answer the following:

1. How attached are you to your pets?

little   1   2   3   4   5   6   7   8   very much

2. How affected are you (will you be) when your pet dies?

little   1   2   3   4   5   6   7   8   very much

3. What is the expected life span of your pet? _____

4. Rate the degree of concern you have about other people's reaction to your feelings when your pet dies.

little   1   2   3   4   5   6   7   8   very much

5. When my pet dies, I plan to replace it . . .

the next day	the next week	the next month	within three months	within 1 year	never

6. How accepting are you of the idea of euthanasia for your pet?

little   1   2   3   4   5   6   7   8   very much

7. How much do you desire to be present during the euthanizing?

little   1   2   3   4   5   6   7   8   very much

8. Humane Societies usually euthanize within 7 days. How accepting are you of this policy?

little   1   2   3   4   5   6   7   8   very much

9. What will be the final disposition of your pet's body? _____

Responses to the Pet Questionnaire
Listed by Question Items

1. It is common to be very attached to a pet. Pets provide us with unconditional positive regard.

2. If there is any congruence between answer #2 and #1, you might give some serious thought as to why. There should be a positive agreement between attachment and response.

3. Some expected life spans are

   dog—(large 8 to 10 years   cat—(indoor: horses—30 years
        small 10 to 15 years)   10 to 15 years)

   gerbils/hamsters—2 to 3 years   rabbit—7 to 12 years

4. If you responded in the 1 or 2, or 7 or 8, you may want to discuss this further.

5. Replacing pets immediately may trivialize the death and its impact. Never replacing them shows a fear.

6 thru 8. On a national level, 7,000,000 dogs and 6,000,000 cats yearly are euthanized; 3,207 pets are euthanized yearly in a town of 60,000 people.

9. The death of a pet requires some planning. If you plan to bury, do check with local laws and cemeteries. If you plan to euthanize, inquire what the vet does with the body of the pet. If you cremate, you need to plan for display or disposal of the cremains.

Discussion and Reflection:

1. What memories of previous pets were recalled?

   _____

   _____

   _____

2. In responding to these questions, were you moved to take any action or change any attitudes? If so, what?

   _____

   _____

   _____

CHAPTER 3

ENCOUNTERING DEATH IN THE CULTURE

3. CULTURE

This chapter deals with our thoughts and feelings about death as they are influenced by our culture. The word "culture" may be a bit threatening. Culture, as we use it here implies the shared assumptions, meanings, and teachings that make up a given society. Culture, we believe, is everything around us. It has to do with food we eat, clothes we wear, TV and movies we watch, and stories we tell each other. It comes to us in our parents' attitudes and admonitions as well as in the cartoon section of the Sunday paper. In a sense, it is the informational environment that surrounds us.

The authors' view of culture is one in which we see a living, dynamic swirl of information ebbing and flowing around us all the time. We are so close to our culture (and it is so close to us) that we may not be fully aware of its influence. A philosophic wag is said to have remarked, "I don't know who discovered water, but I am certain it wasn't fish." While the joke may be a bit vague, it does alert us to the idea that what we take for granted, a natural part of our lives, is hard to step away from to analyze. Culture is to human beings what water is to fish. It surrounds us to such an extent that we don't even notice. This seems particularly true of the cultural messages we get about death.

Activities in this chapter are designed to sharpen the reader's sensitivity to these cultural messages that sometimes shout, sometimes whisper to us about death. The guidelines regarding any understanding of culture, whether one's own or another person's, are straight forward and simple.

First, we urge a respectful attitude toward cultural diversity. Not everyone comes from the same cultural background. Indeed, one of the defining characteristics of the United States of America is that its citizens are made up of a diverse selection of many cultures of the world. Some originating within the boundaries of the nation itself and others from the opposite side of the globe. We can too easily dismiss or make fun of beliefs and traditions that are different from our own. However, with an attitude of openness and respect, our own sense of appreciation can be expanded and enriched when we learn about the cultural heritage of others.

Second, within a framework of respect, we invite careful questioning and re-examination of one's cultural heritage. In fact, in the spirit of constructive criticism we invite you to temporarily assume that some of your cultural influences may be "excess baggage" and to temporarily set them aside for close examination. If after such examination you decide they are worthwhile, you will be more comfortable in their use. For example, one may not choose a certain funeral practice, yet accept it as an honest expression for another. These activities in Chapter 3 will invite, if not provoke, a closer scrutiny of your cultural heritage.

Third, we encourage you to be an active and immediate resource to others in the class as you share your ideas and feelings. The imprint of one's own cultural experience can be a rich resource for others as they struggle to put their own thoughts and feelings into perspective. The immediacy and spontaneity of you-as-a-person and a living example of your heritage can far surpass a book or a lecture about the topic. Classmates can supply "figure and ground," similarities and differences for each other, in which learning comes alive in a cross-cultural comparison and appreciation.

Fourth, we invite an openness to thoughts and feelings in this experiential learning. Death can be a frightening topic in America where death is often hidden and denied. We encourage the examination of one's cultural heritage. Such an examination requires courage as one ventures into previously unchallenged assumptions about death and dying.

Activity 3.1
POETRY

Purpose: To express some poetic thoughts about death.

Time: 30 minutes

Activity Procedure:

1. Using the following letters, write your own poetry, expressing your thoughts and feelings. Let each letter begin the word in that line of your poetry.

    D

    E

    A

    T

    H
    _____

    G

    R

    I

    E

    F
    _____

2. Using Kubler-Ross' stages of death and dying and/or Worden's tasks of mourning, assign the poems you have written to one of the stages or tasks.

Kubler-Ross (stages of death and dying)	Worden (tasks of mourning)
denial	accept the reality of the loss
anger	experience the pain of grief
bargaining	adjust to a world in which the deceased is missing
depression	withdraw emotional energy from the deceased and reinvest in new relationships
acceptance	
(Source: *On Death and Dying* E. Kubler-Ross)	(Source: *Grief Counseling and Grief Therapy*, W.J. Worden)

3. Meet in small groups of four to read and discuss your poetry.

4. Rejoin the entire class to discuss both the poetry and the stages of death and dying plus the tasks of mourning.

Discussion and Reflection:

1. What did your poems reveal to you? _____

   _____

   _____

2. Did your classifications surprise you? Were they at different stages or tasks than you thought they would be?

   _____

   _____

   _____

3. Did your group members agree or disagree with your own classifications? Why might this be so?

   _____

   _____

   _____

4. Give some thought to the particular poem or poems you read. Why did you select that particular poem?

   _____

   _____

   _____

Activity 3.2
THEME POETRY

Purpose: To explore the grief process through poetry.

Time: 30 minutes

Activity Procedure:

1. Using the following letters, write a poem about your feeling and thoughts. Be ready to share them. Let each letter begin that line of poetry.

    H

    E

    A

    L

    I

    N

    G
    _____

    H

    O

    P

    E
    _____

2. Share your poems with one another in small groups.

Discussion and Reflection:

1. What differences did you find in your own poems comparing the "healing" one to the "hope" one?

    _____
    _____
    _____

2. What differences did you find in others?

_____

_____

_____

3. Which was more powerful for you? Why?

_____

_____

_____

4. Choose a few poems to read aloud to the rest of the class. List the ones you selected.

_____

_____

_____

Activity 3.3
PHASES OF DEATH

Purpose: To explore how our language influences the way we think about death.

Time: 20 minutes

Activity Procedure:

1. Following each word or phrase describe the attitude and/or influence implied.

    a. called to a final reward _____

    b. bit the dust _____

    c. bought the farm _____

    d. departed _____

    e. shakin' hands with the devil _____

    f. living in box city _____

    g. lying in state _____

    h. pushin' daisies _____

    i. passed away _____

    j. gone over _____

2. Summarize your feelings as a result of having completed Item 1.

    _____
    _____
    _____
    _____

Discussion and Reflection:

1. What feelings are evoked by each word or phrase?

    _____
    _____
    _____

2. Consider these phrases being used to describe the death of someone you love. What feelings are evoked?

_____

_____

_____

3. What might be the explanations for the origin or use of these phrases?

_____

_____

_____

Activity 3.4
ANECDOTES
(short account of interesting or humorous events)

Purpose: To understand that humor around death may be instructive and/or destructive.

Time: 15 minutes

Activity Procedure:

1. Realize that anecdotes may be marvelous glimpses into human behavior. They can provide us with a rich source of memories. Some can be instructive; others funny; others mean and destructive.

2. Use this page to write down an anecdote that either happened to you or to someone you know. It may be funny, bizarre, odd, or wistfully humorous.

_____
_____
_____
_____
_____
_____
_____
_____
_____
_____
_____
_____
_____
_____
_____
_____

Discussion and Reflection:

1. What is special about the story to you or to the teller?

_____
_____
_____

2. What was instructive about it in your understanding of death?

_____
_____
_____

3. What was funny now that wasn't then?

_____

_____

_____

4. Or what was funny then, but looking back is not?

_____

_____

_____

5. Share this anecdote and your reaction to it with another member of the class.

_____

_____

_____

Activity 3.5
THE GOOD NEWS NEWSPAPER

Purpose: To discover what journalistic responsibility and editorial policy could be concerning death.

Time: 15 minutes

Activity Procedure:

1. Assume that you are the editor of an experimental newspaper. Your editorial policy is to print all the news, but to do it in such a way so as to make it sound good. You are now about to publish the first issue but have run into trouble on the obituary page. You know that you are not allowed to use phrases and words such as: funeral, obituary, death, die, killed, etc.

2. With the help of other class members, layout and write articles about death, deaths of important people, disasters, murder, etc. without using any of the harsh, real words surrounding death. (include ads for funeral homes, crematories, and cemeteries)

Give your examples below:

THE DAILY GAZETTE

| VOL. 114—NO. 264 ☆☆ | ANYTOWN, USA, DAY, DATE, YEAR | © YEAR The Daily Gazette | 25 cents |

Add
Picture
of
Your
Choice

Discussion and Reflection:

1. Would articles like this be better in real newspapers?

   _____

   _____

   _____

2. Would they be easier on their readers?

   _____

   _____

   _____

3. Would this instead be more cruel in the long run? Why?

   _____

   _____

   _____

4. Now look at current daily newspapers, how accurately do they report death related events? Do they gloss over the reality of those events?

   _____

   _____

   _____

Activity 3.6
MOVIES

Purpose: To become more aware of death themes in film.

Time: 20 minutes

Activity Procedure:

1. Identify films and/or TV stories that you have seen recently.

   _____
   _____
   _____

2. Answer the following questions based on films and TV stories identified in Item 1.

   a. How have they portrayed death? _____

      _____
      _____

   b. When was death humorous? _____

      _____
      _____

   c. When was it tragic? _____

      _____
      _____

   d. When was it justified? _____

      _____
      _____

   e. Which films or episodes within the film helped you better understand death and grief?

      _____
      _____
      _____

3. Share some of these movie scenes with other class members.

4. In your memory of films, what level of presentation of death did you most remember? Circle one:

   a. sensitivity   c. accuracy
   b. violence   d. superficiality

Discussion and Reflection:

1. How did your experience match the experience of others in your group?

   _____

   _____

   _____

2. What did you learn about the presentation of death in films and TV, and societal attitudes toward death and dying?

   _____

   _____

   _____

Activity 3.7
EUPHEMISMS

Purpose: To become more sensitive about the euphemisms in our death vocabulary.

Time: 20 minutes

Activity Procedure:

1. Recognize that our language is full of euphemisms.

2. Generate as many as you can think of.

Euphemisms	Harsh Words	Institutional

Examples:
 	
    passed away
    kicked the bucket
	waste 'em	expired

3. Compare your list with others in your group and in the class to compile a master list on the board.

Discussion and Reflection:

1. What justification do we have in using these words?

_____

_____

_____

2. When are we not justified in using these words?

_____

_____

_____

3. What do you think are the purpose of using these words?

_____

_____

_____

Activity 3.8
SYMBOLS OF DEATH

Purpose: To become familiar with the symbols of death.

Time: 15 minutes

Activity Procedure:

1. In the space provided, list and draw some symbols of death that have meaning for you.

Symbol	Degree of Comfort/Harshness		
Meaningful to You	Harsh	0 1 2 3 4 5	Comfort
Meaningful to Others	Harsh	0 1 2 3 4 5	Comfort

2. In the space provided above, list and draw some symbols of death that have meaning to others.

3. To the right of each symbol listed in Items 1 and 2, check the degree of comfort/harshness you have toward the symbols drawn.

Discussion and Reflection:

1. What role do symbols play for us?

_____

_____

_____

2. Were there any symbols that people in your group or class saw differently? How?

_____

_____

_____

3. Which symbols were culturally specific, universal?

_____

_____

_____

Activity 3.9
PERSONAL SYMBOLS

Purpose: To discover one's personal symbols of death.

Time: 10 minutes

Activity Procedure:

1. On this page, draw some personal symbols of death or grieving.

2. Get together with one or two others and share your drawings.

Discussion and Reflection:

1. What was significant about what you drew?

   _____

   _____

   _____

2. Tell the story behind the symbol.

   _____

   _____

   _____

3. List and talk about the feelings you had while completing this activity.

   _____

   _____

   _____

Activity 3.10
HISTORICAL EVENTS

Purpose: To examine the influence of historical events on our attitudes toward death and dying.

Time: 30 minutes

Activity Procedure:

1. In class, generate a list of historical events which are death related or have death related themes: e.g., WW I; Vietnam War; Lincoln Assassination; Kennedy Assassination; holocaust; the plague; etc.

2. In small groups of 5, place the events on the grid provided on the next page.

3. Discuss and record the groups answers to the events in the space provided.

4. Return to the class for reports from each group.

Discussion and Reflection:

1. What historical events influenced you personally?

   _____

   _____

   _____

2. What modern event has the look of a historical event that will be seen by historians as a changing point?

   _____

   _____

   _____

3. Where did members of the class disagree on what constituted a historical event?

   _____

   _____

   _____

EVENT	Questions		
	What meaning was assigned to the event when it occurred?	How did this event influence history?	How is the event viewed in the present?

Activity 3.11
LYRICS

"Music a thing as seasonable in grief as in joy"

Bishop Richard Hooker, 1594

Purpose: To review how the music arts depict death and grief.

Time: 20 minutes

Activity Procedure:

1. In small groups, generate song titles that fit these various categories:

NATURAL DEATHS	ACCIDENTAL DEATHS	SUICIDES	HOMICIDES
example: Song for Duke	Big Bad John	Save the Life of My Child	Frankie and Johnny

2. Share your list with the class.

3. As the class discusses titles, add to your list.

Discussion and Reflection:

1. What do the words signify?

_____

_____

_____

2. How do they help tell the story?

_____

_____

_____

3. How do they help the listener understand the death?

_____

_____

_____

4. What is their attitude toward the death?

_____

_____

_____

Activity 3.14
CHRISTMAS

Purpose: To plan a holiday routine after a death so that it is balanced between grief and joy.

Time: 30 minutes

Activity Procedure:

1. Assume that Christmas is near, and a recent death is remembered.

2. Identify who is to be included in this day's events.

3. List things you would like to have around.

4. Identify customs, rituals, or meaningful acts that you what to include.

5. Plan, in the space provided, how the day should go so that it recognizes the death and still frees you for the rest of the day.

   Please allow for:
   time to grieve
   time to remember
   time to celebrate

TIME	PEOPLE	THINGS	EVENTS
MORNING:			
AFTERNOON:			
EVENING:			

Discussion and Reflection:

1. How realistic is this plan?

   _____

   _____

   _____

2. What would it feel like at the end of the day?

   _____

   _____

   _____

3. What feelings did you have about acknowledging a death on Christmas?

   _____

   _____

   _____

Activity 3.15
ACKNOWLEDGING GRIEF

Purpose: To plan a symbolic day that will be meaningful to you as you grieve.

Time: 30 minutes

Activity Procedure:

1. Assume that one of your personal symbolic days is near.

2. Plan how that day should go so that it recognizes the death and still acknowledges the time you need for yourself.

TIME	PEOPLE	THINGS	EVENTS
MORNING:			
AFTERNOON:			
EVENING:			

Discussion and Reflection:

1. How realistic is the plan?

   _____

   _____

   _____

2. What sense of resistance did you feel in planning for the day? What was the source of your resistance?

   _____

   _____

   _____

3. Consider if there is any advantage to facing death directly as this activity proposes?

   _____

   _____

   _____

Activity 3.16
DRAW DEATH

Purpose: To use non-verbal expression for identifying our thoughts and feelings about death.

Materials: colored pencils, markers, crayons

Time: 20 minutes

Background Information:

Sometimes we use the intellect to protect us from our feelings about death. For some people, art is a more direct expression of emotions. As you draw death, try to be aware of what happens to you. Don't let this exercise intimidate you. Be expressive, risky; try impressions and symbols, etc.

Activity Procedure:

1. Draw death.

2. Use color or colors as you wish.

Discussion and Reflection:

1. How did this exercise get you beyond the intellect?

   _____

   _____

   _____

2. If you used colors, what significance did they have for you?

   _____

   _____

   _____

3. What symbols did you use?

   _____

   _____

   _____

4. Share your drawing with others in the group.

5. What parallels did you see with others? What differences?

   _____

   _____

   _____

CHAPTER 4

ENCOUNTERING DEATH IN INSTITUTIONS

4. INSTITUTIONS

Human beings and institutions have had an uneasy relationship throughout history. No society exists without its institutions which serve to formally transmit values, enforce those values, and, to some extent, resist change within a society. One of the consequences of the technological revolution, the movement toward an urbanized society, a highly mobile population, and a decreased reliance upon the nuclear family has been the rise in importance of institutions in death and dying.

For many people still living in this society they can remember when death was not an isolated and distant event in the lives of a community. People died younger only a few years ago. Infant mortality was higher. Death was not so unexpected. When these deaths occurred, they were often at home. The funeral directors would come to the home and make the preparation for the funeral in the home. Physicians might even have been in attendance in the home. Communities were smaller and families were geographically closer. Support for family members was more likely to come from nearby relatives and neighbors.

In America today, frequently the death occurs in a hospital attended by strangers. Death may come suddenly and family members may not be able to travel the great distances that often separate loved ones. Grandparents may be in a retirement community, in a nursing home, or have stayed in their family home while children and grandchildren moved to distant parts of the nation. Even if a neighbor hears that someone's parent has died no strong connection is made with the person who has died. Showing care for the family through comfort giving actions such as bringing over food, caring for farm animals, doing chores, or minding the store are no longer possible since that world has disappeared for so many of us. Today the task would be much more difficult as we try to fill in at the factory or help finish the computer program. Much of what was once done by family and friends now falls to institutions. While we once learned of the death of a friend or loved one by a neighbor and by word-of-mouth, now we are informed by police officers or hospital personnel. We learn of the death of a neighbor in the newspaper. The death occurs in a hospital and the body is moved directly to a mortuary. Funerals or cremations are conducted by professionals in these fields and the family may be little involved.

A death involves many institutions in modern American life. The list includes hospitals, churches, police, ambulance service, nursing homes, funeral homes, cemeteries, and others. Some institutions such as Hospice, have been created to make death and dying less distant and aloof. In many ways, Hospice strives to create a more peaceful death by trying to open communication between the dying person and friends and family members—to make death and dying more personal and less institutional.

This is an area of modern life with which we must make our peace. One may dream but doing so is unrealistic when we dream that our lives will become less mobile, that the nuclear family will regain its geographical closeness, that communities will become less urbanized and more knowledgeable of one another. In today's world we appear to be growing more complex and in the midst of these changes, we have to somehow learn to use our institutions to help us stay close with our loved one's when they are dying. Will institutions gain more control of death and dying? Is there a way to use institutions to provide for personal closeness and concern during dying? Is it possible to maintain family values in the face of the increasing institutionalization of America? These questions and others represent some of the challenges facing us as we encounter death and institutions.

Activity 4.1
HOW WE FEEL ABOUT INSTITUTIONS

Purpose: To realize that we have feelings about institutions and the people who work in them.

Time: 20 minutes

Activity Procedure:

1. Remember back to a death you, your family, or a close friend experienced.

2. Place a check mark to the left of each institution involved in some way with that death.

3. Do the same of people involved.

4. Use the following list of feelings and to the right of each institution and person/ people involved, write the feeling you remember having or that you experienced from a family member or friend. (A list of feelings is provided on the next page.)

INSTITUTIONS	FEELINGS	PEOPLE	FEELINGS
Church/Synagogue		Police	
Hospital		Doctor	
Military		Nurse	
Police		Paramedics	
Social Services		Clergy	
Funeral Home		Funeral Director	
Nursing Home		Counselor	
Cemetery		Insurance salesperson Coroner	
Insurance Company			
Media		Mental Health	
Red Cross		Ambulance Service	
Hospice			
Others (specify)		Others (specify)	

FEELINGS

awe	gratitude	resentful
admiration	guilty	sadness
ambivalent	hurt	security
anger	irritated	suspicious
affection	joyful	trust
confusion	pleased	Others (List)
curious	outrage	_____
frightened	questioning	_____
frustration	relief	_____

Discussion and Reflection:

1. In summary what are your feelings toward these institutions and people?

_____

_____

_____

2. Compare your list for similarities and differences to other members of the class.

_____

_____

_____

3. What conclusions can you reach about how our institutions deal with death?

_____

_____

_____

4. Did you find a difference between your emotions toward the institutions than toward the people who work in them?

_____

_____

_____

Activity 4.2
ECONOMICS

Purpose: To identify those institutions which profit financially, directly or indirectly, from deaths.

Time: 20 minutes

Activity Procedure:

1. Have each member of the class name a profession that profits from death and list it on the board.

2. Discuss how each profits from death.

3. Recategorize the list into three lists—those which directly profit, those which profit indirectly, and those that exploit death.

Profits Directly	Profits Indirectly	Exploits Death

4. Review the list of institutions and check how you perceive each as profiting from death.

INSTITUTION	PROFITS DIRECTLY	PROFITS INDIRECTLY	EXPLOITS DEATH
Hospitals			
Hospice			
Church/Synagogue			
Military			
Police			
Social Services			
Cemetery			
Insurance Companies			
Doctors			
Lawyers			
Tax Agencies			
Crematory			
TV/Movie			
Media Mental			
Health Workers			
Red Cross Agencies			
Ambulance Services			
Support Groups			
Nursing Homes			
Paramedics			
Nurses			
Newspapers			
Others (specify)			
_____			
_____			

Discussion and Reflection:

1. Does it bother you to think that institutions can profit from deaths. Why or why not?

   _____

   _____

   _____

2. Which institutions profit the most? Why?

   _____

   _____

   _____

3. Are there agencies dealing with death that do not profit and, if so, give examples?

   _____

   _____

   _____

4. Identify the various feelings you experienced as you categorized professions.

   _____

   _____

   _____

Activity 4.3
CARE FOR THE DYING

Purpose: To discover the role an ideal agency could provide for the dying and their families.

Time: 15 minutes

Activity Procedure:

1. Create an institution that would care for the dying and their families.

2. Identify goals and objectives of caring.

   a. _____
   b. _____
   c. _____

3. Identify goals for the dying person.

   a. _____
   b. _____
   c. _____

4. List goals for the family.

   a. _____
   b. _____
   c. _____

5. List goals for the staff.

   a. _____
   b. _____
   c. _____

6. Compare your institution, and its standards with those of hospice institutions nationwide. "Standards of Care for a Model Hospice" are provided on pages that follow so that you can compare.

Discussion and Reflection:

1. What were the similarities and differences between your goals and national hospice standards?

   _____
   _____

2. How widely practiced are your ideal standards in your community?

   _____
   _____

3. Do you feel comforted knowing that hospices exist? Why?

   _____
   _____

STANDARDS OF CARE FOR A MODEL HOSPICE

Basic Standards

1. The needs of all involved must be taken into account, this includes family, staff, and patient.
2. As much as possible, the terminally ill patient is allowed to have control and power in decision making.

Patient-Oriented Goals

1. Symptom control is a priority.
2. Alleviation of pain is a priority.
3. A "living will" or "no code" request by the patient is taken into account as part of care.
4. A secure, comfortable, and warm environment is expected.
5. If in residential care, the patient, when possible, should be encouraged to visit home. Otherwise, patient is encouraged to maintain some sort of activity as long as possible.

Family (Primary Caregiver) Oriented Goals

1. A comfortable atmosphere developed to discuss issues related to death and personal needs.
2. Private space and time allotted during visits.
3. Private time and space allowed immediately after death of patient.

Staff-Oriented Goals

1. Professional staff are encouraged to develop relationships with the dying patient and family.
2. Professional staff are encouraged to develop their own network for encouragement, support, and education.

NOTE: Loosely adapted from R.J. Kastenbaum (1986), *Death, Society, and Human Experience.* Columbus, OH: Merrill Publishing Company.

Discussion and Reflection:

1. What were the similarities and differences between your goals and national hospice standards?

_____

_____

2. How widely practiced are your ideal standards in your community?

_____

_____

3. Do you feel comforted knowing that hospices exist? Why?

_____

_____

Activity 4.4
CHURCH

Purpose: To understand better the role of rites and rituals of religious institutions.

Time: 20 minutes

Activity Procedure:

1. In small groups recall any formal or informal rites and rituals associated with your religious values that surround death or funerals.

2. List them according to whether they were helpful or not.

RITE OR RITUAL	Helpful	
	Yes	No
1.		
2.		
3.		
4.		
5.		

Discussion and Reflection:

1. What made the difference between a rite or ritual being helpful or not?

   _____

   _____

2. What differences of opinion came up regarding whether a ritual was helpful or not?

   _____

   _____

3. What criteria did you use for your determination?

   _____

   _____

Activity 4.5
NOTIFICATION OF DEATH

Purpose: To increase sensitivity and skill in death notification strategy.

Time: 40 minutes

Activity Procedure:

1. As a whole class, ask for people who have received notification of a death to share how it was done, giving their reactions and constructive criticisms.

2. Next, in small groups of 4 to 6, develop a short training program for "notification of next of kin." What would you include? Don't forget the how's, and the objectives.

_____

_____

_____

_____

_____

_____

3. Have each small group role play a "notification" scene for the rest of the class. First illustrate some of the pitfalls and problems. Then, role play the same situation using the principles and goals from Item 2. Let the other members critique.

Discussion and Reflection:

1. Did one group have some better ideas? How could you incorporate all of the best ideas?

_____

_____

_____

2. Which groups used detachment as a means of dealing with the notification. What are the pros and cons of that method?

_____

_____

_____

3. Which ideas and methods made you the most comfortable? Gave you the most information that you felt necessary? Seemed empathic?

_____

_____

_____

CHAPTER 5

ENCOUNTERING UNEXPECTED DEATHS

5. UNEXPECTED DEATH

When a death occurs, it is often considered "natural." When someone dies after a long life, then, while the pain is still present, understanding and logical mental processing often occurs. When we know a death is coming we can "make arrangements." We can write wills, settle financial affairs, contact relatives, and even say good-bye to loved ones. We can bring some order to the chaos a death can bring. Even expected death brings shock and disbelief. What is more shocking and more difficult to deal with is unexpected death.

Psychologists tell us that one of the characteristics of human beings is a desire to order things, to bring control to their lives, to finish unfinished tasks. Many experiments have demonstrated this characteristic. For some reason, human beings don't like the incomplete. Nor do we like the unexpected. This human characteristic is what seems to make unexpected death so difficult to cope with.

Unexpected death catches us unprepared. We are unprepared in the common tasks of death (selecting a funeral home, deciding on burial or cremation, notifying people). We are unprepared emotionally.

Unexpected death is unnatural. It destroys our sense of control. It defies our sense of a just and reasonable world. Unexpected death can leave us struggling for answers which may never come. The most sought after answer is to the question "Why?."

This category of unexpected deaths is a difficult one. While deaths from accidents, murders, and disasters are unexpected that doesn't mean they are necessarily uncommon. One of the frightening facts of life is that accidents are a leading cause of death. This is especially true of young people. A commonplace occurrence in today's world is to pick up our daily newspaper and read of another automobile accident that has claimed the life of one or more people. No comfort exists in the idea that accidents are common. They are still unexpected and they attack the flow of our lives. We are stunned, shocked, and unprepared.

While automobile, swimming, or mountain climbing accidents stun us as individuals, some accidents shock us because of the number of people who have died. Earthquakes, floods, fires, airline crashes, and other disasters become even more incomprehensible. Understanding the death of tens, hundreds, or thousands of people at once is beyond us. We cannot seem to grasp the loss of an entire block of neighbors. We cannot comprehend the idea that an entire village has disappeared.

We cannot come to terms with the death of numbers of people who may exceed the entire population of the town in which we live. For some, the term "act of God," which these disasters are often called, may add to the contradiction and difficulty dealing with the shock and horror of such experiences.

Finally, the one area of unexpected death that is so frightening to us is murder. Experts in law enforcement tell us that the nature of murder has changed over the years. While not much relief comes from the knowledge, murder was once a much more personal affair than it appears to be now. It was once predictable that murder was more closely linked to people we knew. Murders were "crimes of passion." The danger now is that increasingly murders are happening between people unknown to each other. Again, a not uncommon occurrence is to pick up a newspaper and read that some person has been killed in an act of random violence or even by politically motivated terrorism. A jogger will be shot from a passing car. A mother killed in her living room by someone shooting into the house. A store owner or convenience store clerk killed for no apparent reason during a robbery.

New words enter our vocabulary in an attempt to describe what is happening in our society. Gangs go "wilding" in violent rampages, in their explanations, to counteract the boredom of their lives. This new form of murder frightens and threatens our understanding of the world. What preparations can we make to ensure the continuity of our lives? How can we protect those we love from random acts of violence? Who can we trust? All of these questions may not have answers. Still, unexpected death can be encountered. We may not be able to prepare ourselves in any way other than intellectually. While the intention of the authors is not to create the emotions of unexpected death, the intention of this chapter is to provide activities which asks each of the readers to confront the issue of unexpected death in life.

Activity 5.1
HOW DISASTERS AFFECT US

Purpose: To recognize the magnitude of deaths by disaster and to assess its effect on us.

Time: 20 Minutes

Activity Procedures:

1. As a class, list on the board at least 10 disasters with which the class members are familiar.

2. Have each member of the class choose five of the 10 disasters and arrange those on the graph provided below.

3. Make the arrangement reflect how "close or distant" one feels from the event.

4. Discuss your individual responses in the class.

HOW DISASTERS AFFECT US

Disaster	very close								very distant	
_____	1	2	3	4	5	6	7	8	9	10
_____	1	2	3	4	5	6	7	8	9	10
_____	1	2	3	4	5	6	7	8	9	10
_____	1	2	3	4	5	6	7	8	9	10
_____	1	2	3	4	5	6	7	8	9	10

Discussion and Reflection:

1. What criteria did you use for establishing distance (geographically, chronologically, etc.)?

   _____

   _____

   _____

2. What responses to the disasters did you see?

   _____

   _____

   _____

3. Has anyone you know been killed in a disaster?   Yes _____   No _____
   If so, would you share the story with the class.

   _____

   _____

   _____

4. Have you or anyone you know survived a disaster?   Yes _____   No _____
   If so, would you share the story with the class?

   _____

   _____

   _____

Activity 5.2
MURDER AND GRIEF

Purpose: To learn about the grief process as it affects survivors.

Time: 30 minutes

Background Information:

The four stages of the mourning process are

Stage 1—Shock and numbness
Duration is generally 48 hrs to 2 weeks

Stage 2—Searching and Yearning
Duration is often from second week to 4 months

Stage 3—Reorganization
Duration is often from about the 4th month through the 7th month

Stage 4—Disorientation
Often is from about the 7th month through the 24th month

These time spans vary considerably from individual to individual.

Behavioral characteristics often overlap during mourning.

Survivors of a homicide death may find that trials and news coverage may prolong the first three stages.

Activity Procedure:

1. Review and discuss the information related to the four stages of the mourning process.

2. Classify each of the following 25 characteristics associated with the mourning process as to one of the four stages.

CHARACTERISTICS	STAGES			
	1	2	3	4
a. resists input (trying to find shelter)				
b. very sensitive to stimuli				
c. disorganized				
d. sense of release				
e. renewed energy				
f. strong urge to flee setting of loss				
g. testing what is real				
h. stunned feelings				
i. trying to live as if nothing has happened				
j. low compliance with doctor's orders and other expectations				
k. feeling uncertain				
l. judgment-making difficult, concentration limited				
m. depressed				
n. guilt				
o. weight loss/gain, more than 10 lbs.				
p. stable sleeping and eating habits				
q. temptation to see mourning as a disease				
r. anger				
s. restless, impatient				
t. functioning impeded (zombie, robot)				
u. emotional outbursts				
v. oversensitivity of reality and consequences				
w. time of turning to physicians				
x. psychosomatic dimension				
y. makes judgements more easily				

3. Compare your answers with those of the authors. (Authors' answers are at the end of this activity.)

Discussion and Reflection:

1. Discuss with others the differences between your classification of characteristics from those of the authors.

   _____

   _____

   _____

2. How do these differ from the other stages of grief of natural deaths?

   _____

   _____

   _____

3. Do you have any basic disagreements with the stage model provided in this activity?

   _____

   _____

   _____

4. Do you have any personal stories that can be shared?

   _____

   _____

   _____

Authors' Answers to Activity Procedure Item 2

Stage 1.   a, h, l, t, u

Stage 2.   b, g, k, r, s

Stage 3.   c, f, i, j, m, n, o, q, v, w, x

Stage 4.   d, e, p, y

Activity 5.3
SURVIVING DISASTER

Purpose: To provide information about surviving and survivors of disasters.

Time: 15 minutes

Activity Procedure:

1. As an individual, respond to the "Surviving Disaster True-False Test" below.

2. Divide into groups of six and discuss your answers. As you do, use the "Surviving Disaster True-False Test Responses" supplied on a following page.

SURVIVING DISASTER TRUE-FALSE TEST

1. T F Persons who have survived a disaster in which others have died have special concerns in grieving.

2. T F Persons who have survived a disaster are survivors twice over.

3. T F Person who have survived a disaster experience no guilt about their survival.

4. T F Adequate warning of a known impending disaster can save lives.

5. T F Meeting the physical needs of the survivors is the only concern of disaster teams.

6. T F When people have been drowned or buried alive in a disaster it doesn't make much sense to dig them up or find them only to have to bury them again.

7. T F People who lose only material possessions feel guilty.

8. T F Many surviving victims resolve their grief more quickly because they realize they could have done nothing to change it.

9. T F Those who are helpers during a disaster (emergency crews, rescue workers, counselors) are also vulnerable to the emotional impact of the event.

10. T F After a disaster, business and corporations should make adjustment for bills, debts, and payments.

SURVIVING DISASTER TRUE-FALSE TEST RESPONSES

1. _T_ Persons who have survived a disaster in which others were killed have special concerns in grieving including guilt, reliving the experience, disturbed sleep, nightmares, and other problems in living.

2. _T_ Persons who have survived a disaster are survivors twice over because they survived an event which could have ended their lives and, possibly, they have survived the death of friends, relatives, and neighbors.

3. _F_ There is usually guilt about being lucky, undeserving, old, young, or some other reason over which they do not understand their own survival.

4. _T_ There are numerous examples where warnings have saved lives. For example, weather warning such as flood and tornado warnings. The Mount St. Helens Volcano in Washington resulted in relatively few deaths because of warnings. Other smaller volcanic explosions have caused many more deaths because of lack of warning.

5. _F_ The emotional needs of survivors should not be neglected.

6. _F_ It is important that survivors identify the deceased. It seems clear that the recovery of the body of a loved one can aid the grieving process.

7. _T_ They feel guilty for mourning their material loss when others have lost family members.

8. _F_ Many people feel anxious, vulnerable, fearful, and depressed for long periods. In some cases old problems related to personal or relationship issues re-emerge.

9. _T_ Indeed, they need some of the same emotional support as do survivors. This is especially true if the victims are infants or if the disaster results in situations for which the helpers are unprepared or untrained.

10. _T_ In fact, business and corporations who do allow for leniency and show understanding help defuse some of the anger and become an aid in the grieving process.

Discussion and Reflection:

1. Were some questions more difficult than others? Why?

_____

_____

_____

2. Do you disagree with any of the answers given? Which ones?

_____

_____

_____

Activity 5.4
ACCIDENTAL DEATHS

Purpose: To be aware of the frequency of accidents causing deaths and to realize their impact on the grieving process.

Time: 30 minutes

Activity and Procedure:

1. As an individual, look at the chart below and search your memory to find any accidental deaths with which you are familiar. Record the deaths by type and sex. Cite the incident (use few words or phrases).

ACCIDENT			YOUR INDIVIDUAL RESPONSE	GROUP	
Related to	**Sex** **M**	**F**	**Incident**	**Frequency** **M**	**F**
Air					
Auto/Motorcycle Bicycle					
Climbing Hiking					
Drugs					
Guns					
Occupation					
Pedestrian					
Sports					
Water					
Other (specify)					

2. Divide into groups of four to recall and share any memories you desire in the small group.

3. In the last two columns of the chart, tally the kind of accidents with which the group has personal knowledge that have taken a life. Note whether the person who died was male or female.

4. In the whole class, tally the frequency of deaths by accident.

Discussion and Reflection:

1. Were you surprised at the number of accidents you remembered? Did not remember?

_____

_____

_____

2. Did the class tally surprise you? So many? So few?

_____

_____

_____

3. What emotions emerged as you discussed deaths by accidents?

_____

_____

_____

Activity 5.5
POST-TRAUMATIC REACTIONS

Purpose: To acquaint the reader with the idea that grief may be uncomplicated (normal and expected) or complicated (grief that continuously and for an extended period of time interferes with normal living).

Time: 15 minutes

Activity Procedure:

1. As an individual, respond to the Forced Choice Test provided.

POST-TRAUMATIC REACTIONS FORCED CHOICE TEST

Which of the following symptoms are considered to be indicative of a complicated grief reaction.

1. a. A diminishing frequency of memories of the event.
   b. A persistent and continuous memory of the event.

2. a. Intermittent dreams of the event.
   b. Recurrent, detailed, and frequent dreams of the event.

3. a. Re-living the experience.
   b. Remembering the experience.

4. a. Recollections marked by sadness to places, dates and situations related to the event.
   b. Severe anxiety reactions to places, dates and situations related to the event.

5. a. Resistance to thoughts or feelings of the event.
   b. Hesitancy to thoughts or feelings of the event.

6. a. Avoiding activities or situations that remind one of the event.
   b. Discomfort to activities or situations that remind one of the event.

7. a. Loss of memory of important details of the event.
   b. Difficulty in remembering important details of the event.

8. a. Postponement or delay of interest in work, household tasks, and other responsibilities.
   b. Extended loss of interest in work, household tasks, and other responsibilities.

9. a. Breakdown in interpersonal relationships.
   b. Stress in interpersonal relationships.

10. a. Dampened use of feelings.
    b. Inflexibility in use of feelings (repetitive and/or inappropriate).

11. a. Sad anticipation of the future.
    b. Personal sense of doom.

12. a. Intermittent sleep disturbance.
    b. Persistent sleep disturbance.

13. a. Constant irritability and/or anger.
    b. Occasional irritability and/or anger.

14. a. Unremitting difficulty in concentration.
    b. Shortened attention span.

15. a. Heightened caution.
    b. Constant guardedness and suspiciousness.

2. When the test is completed, divide into sub-groups of approximately 5 each to discuss the individual answers.

3. In the small group, score your individual test. The correct responses are as follows:

UA = Uncomplicated Grief
PTG = Post-traumatic Grief

Item	UG	PTG
1	a	b
2	a	b
3	b	a
4	a	b
5	b	a
6	b	a
7	b	a
8	a	b

Item	UG	PTG
9	b	a
10	a	b
11	a	b
12	a	b
13	b	a
14	b	a
15	a	b

Total (PTG) _____

If an individual has six or more of the reactions that are shown as post-traumatic grief, that person probably could benefit from seeing a professional counselor or therapist.

4. Discuss the suggested answers in the small group.

Discussion and Reflection:

1. Did you have any problems selecting the complicated grief responses? If you did, why might that be so?

_____

_____

_____

2. Were the grief reactions indicated as normal and uncomplicated more serious than you had anticipated?

_____

_____

3. What emotional reaction did you have to the normal, expected, and uncomplicated grief reaction.

_____

_____

_____

Activity 5.6
CAUSE OF DEATH

Purpose: To illustrate the death rate of one cause of death.

Time: 5 minutes

Activity Procedure:

1. What does this graph represent?

2. Consult the answer section of this book.

Discussion and Reflection:

1. Recognizing that these numbers* are for people in U.S. killed by guns in one week, do these statistics alarm you? Why or why not?

_____

_____

_____

2. What changes would you propose, if any, to help reduce this statistic?

_____

_____

_____

3. Compared to other countries, the U.S. rates unusually high in this statistic? Why do you think this is so?

_____

_____

_____

*Time Magazine (July 17, 1989) calculated that in one typical week 464 people were killed by guns. This included homocides, suicides, and accidents. The figure on the prior page is a graphical reproduction of these statistics.

CHAPTER 6

ENCOUNTERING SUICIDE

6. SUICIDE

Suicide has been a concern of humanity throughout history. Different cultures have responded to suicide in different ways. Some with horror and distain and others with honor and pride. Questions surrounding suicide can be as lofty as philosophy and theology and as personal as the death of a father, mother, or child. In truth, deaths by suicide are both matters of concern for the entire society and for individuals. Society, as a whole, must find ways of educating about suicide, creating agencies to cope with the victims of suicide, and preventing suicide. Individuals, who must profit from opportunities for education, have other tasks as well. Individuals must confront their values, examine their attitudes, and, ultimately, make peace with their own understanding of suicide. What role does it play in life? Do circumstances exist in which suicide is a reasonable choice? If not, why not? If so, under what circumstances?

These are questions all of us must consider. We must consider them because suicide touches every socio-economic strata, every age group, all educational levels, every profession, all religions, and both genders. While much publicity has been given to the suicide rates of youth, and this has served to draw attention to suicide in our society, the other developmental phases of life are affected by suicide as well. The ages 20 to 40 claim more deaths by suicide than any other age group. The elderly have a percentage rate of suicide far above their numbers in the population.

While men complete suicide more frequently than women, at a rate of about 3 or 4 to 1, women attempt suicide more frequently than men, surprisingly at a rate of about 3 or 4 to 1. One of the danger signs of modern life is that women appear to be approaching men in completed suicides.

Beyond an understanding of the populations who attempt and complete suicide, each of us can become familiar with the causes and symptoms of suicide. Our society seems to hold a number of myths about suicide. In order to be of help to one another, these myths need to be dispelled. One of the activities in this chapter attempts to do just that. Perhaps, one thing we need to know is that what can move a person to suicide need not necessarily be something other people would consider to be a major failure in a person's life. Little things can add up. What is important is to understand that the motives of a person thinking about suicide are vital to him or her, even if they seem trivial to us. All talk of suicide should be taken seriously. That is the first step in suicide prevention. The activities in this chapter are aimed at dispelling myths, identifying symptoms, and providing strategies for prevention. The intention of the authors has been to provide information that will inform and give concrete suggestions for helping if a situation ever arises in which you are called upon to prevent a suicide.

Activity 6.1
ASSESSING OUR OWN ATTITUDES

Purpose: To examine one's own attitudes towards suicide.

Time: 10 minutes

Activity Procedure:

Answer the following by circling the statement that is most nearly correct for you.

1. How comfortable are you in talking about suicide?

   a. very comfortable
   b. somewhat comfortable
   c. somewhat uncomfortable
   d. very uncomfortable

2. What do you need to help you feel more comfortable in your discussion of suicide? Circle all that apply.

   a. books
   b. videos
   c. classes
   d. workshops
   e. knowing a friend who can talk about it
   f. experience in helping someone

3. How comfortable do you feel talking with someone who has expressed suicidal thoughts?

   a. very comfortable
   b. somewhat comfortable
   c. somewhat uncomfortable
   d. very uncomfortable

Discussion and Reflection:

1. Share your feelings and answers with your small group.

2. Discuss the reasons you answered as you did.

3. Did any previous experience color your responses?

   _____

   _____

   _____

Activity 6.2
HOW CLOSE IS SUICIDE?

Purpose: To realize many people have been touched by suicide.

Time: 10 minutes

Activity Procedure:

Fill in the chart below with the number of persons whom you know have had thoughts of suicide, attempted suicide or died by suicide. Then total all of the individual results for the entire class.

Person	Thoughts About Suicide	Attempted Suicide	Died by Suicide
Self			
Family			
Friends			
Classmates			
My Total			
Class Total			

Discussion and Reflection:

1. Did any of the numbers surprise you? If so, which ones?

   _____

   _____

   _____

2. Identify any patterns.

   _____

   _____

   _____

3. What generalizations are fair to make from this?

   _____

   _____

   _____

Activity 6.3
SUICIDE INFORMATION TEST

Purpose: To increase one's information base about suicide.

Time: 20 minutes

Activity Procedure:

Answer the following to the best of your knowledge, then correct your paper with the answers provided at the end of this activity.

SUICIDE INFORMATION TEST

1. Suicide accounts for more than _____ deaths a year in the United States.

    a. 5,000
    b. 10,000
    c. 15,000
    d. 20,000

2. Suicide is the _____ cause of death of college students.

    a. most frequent
    b. second most frequent
    c. third most frequent
    d. fourth most frequent

3. Among medical patients, the group which has the highest suicide rate is . . .

    a. terminally ill
    b. chronically ill

4. The age group most likely to commit suicide is . . .

    a. 15 to 20
    b. 20 to 40
    c. 40 to 60
    d. 60 to 80

5. The profession with the highest suicide rate is . . .

    a. psychologists
    b. nurses
    c. morticians
    d. physicians
    e. statisticians

6. Clues to suicide would most likely be found in . . .

    a. verbal statements
    b. behavioral acts
    c. situational events
    d. all of the above
    e. none of the above

7. The emotion most often associated with suicide is . . .

    a. anger
    b. jealously
    c. depression
    d. frustration

8. Suicide rates are highest among . . .

    a. unmarried, expectant mothers
    b. married, expectant mothers
    c. women who are not pregnant

9. The means most likely to be used in a suicide is . . .

    a. drug overdose
    b. gun
    c. slash wrists
    d. jumping from a high place

10. The best predictor of a suicide attempt is . . .

    a. a family member attempting suicide
    b. reading articles about suicide
    c. a close friend attempting suicide
    d. a previous suicide attempt

11. A condition which increases the likelihood of suicide is . . .

    a. psychosis
    b. alcohol use
    c. drug use
    d. all of the above
    e. none of the above

12. Of the ethnic groups listed, which has the highest suicide rate?

    a. African-Americans
    b. Caucasion
    c. Asians
    d. Hispanics

13. Of the ethnic groups listed, which has the highest suicide rate?

    a. African-Americans
    b. Hispanics
    c. Native Americans
    d. Caucasions

14. Suicide is more likely among the . . .

    a. single, never married
    b. married
    c. divorced or widowed

15. The sex most likely to attempt suicide is _____; the sex most likely to complete suicide is _____.

    a. male
    b. female

Reflection and Discussion:

1. Choose the question which provided you with new information. Reflect on the reason why the information was new.

_____

_____

_____

2. Which questions provoked the most resistance in you? What social, psychological, economic, or other factors combine to make that answer correct?

_____

_____

_____

3. What question was answered incorrectly by most members of the class? Why?

_____

_____

_____

Answers to Suicide Information Test:

1. d,   2. b,   3. b,   4. d,   5. d,   6. d,   7. c,   8. c,   9. b,   10. d,   11. d,   12. b,
13. c,   14. c,   15. b, a.

Activity 6.4
SUICIDE STATISTICS

Purpose: To increase the base of information about the suicide phenomena.

Time: 20 minutes

Activity Procedure:

Answer the "Suicide Statistics Questionnaire" by circling the appropriate statement for each item. Compare your answers with those provided at the end of this activity.

Suicide Statistics Questionnaire

1. Suicide accounts for _____% of all deaths in the United States.

    a. over 1%
    b. over 5%
    c. over 10%
    d. over 15%

2. The region with the highest rate of suicide (per 100,000) is . . .

    a. Pacific
    b. South
    c. Atlantic
    d. Rocky Mountain

3. The region with the lowest rate of suicide is . . .

    a. Pacific
    b. North Central
    c. Mid-Atlantic
    d. Rocky Mountain

4. The state with the highest rate of suicide is . . .

    a. Wyoming
    b. California
    c. New Jersey
    d. Hawaii

5. The state with the lowest rate of suicide is . . .

    a. Wyoming
    b. California
    c. New Jersey
    d. Hawaii

6. The metro-service area (city) with the highest rate of suicide is . . .

    a. Baltimore, MD
    b. San Antonio, TX
    c. Minneapolis-St. Paul, MN
    d. Tampa-St. Petersburg, FL

7. The metro-service area (city) with the lowest rate of suicide is . . .

    a. Seattle-Everett, WA
    b. New York-Newark, NJ
    c. Denver-Boulder, CO
    d. Dallas-Ft. Worth, TX

8. In the United States a person dies by suicide every _____ minutes.

    a. 6
    b. 12
    c. 18
    d. 24

9. For the nation as a whole there are _____ attempts for every suicide.

    a. 4
    b. 20
    c. 100
    d. 200

10. For the elderly, there are _____ attempts for every suicide.

    a. 4
    b. 20
    c. 100
    d. 200

11. For teenagers and college students, there are _____ attempts for every suicide.

    a. 4
    b. 20
    c. 100
    d. 200

12. What percentage of people try to communicate their suicidal intentions to someone?

    a. 25%
    b. 50%
    c. 75%
    d. 95%

13. The number of living Americans who have attempted suicide is about _____.

        a. 2 million
        b. 3 million
        c. 5 million
        d. 7 million

14. The estimate is that each suicide intimately affects at least _____ other people

        a. 1
        b. 3
        c. 6
        d. 10

15. Elderly make up about 12% of the general population in the USA, but account for _____% of all suicides.

        a. 10
        b. 15
        c. 20
        d. 25

Discussion and Reflection:

1. Choose the question which provided you with new information. Reflect on the reasons why this information was new.

    _____

    _____

    _____

2. Which question provoked the most resistance in you? What social, psychological, economic, or other factors combine to make that answer correct?

    _____

    _____

    _____

3. What questions were answered incorrectly by most members of the class? Why?

    _____

    _____

    _____

Answers to Suicide Statistics Questionnaire:

The following answers were extracted from the National Center for Health Statistics (1987), Hyattsville, MD, "Advanced Report of Final Mortality Statistics 1985," v. 36 #5 supplement.

1. _a_ The actual figure is 1.4% of total deaths are from suicide and is ranked eighth for all causes of death.

2. _d_ Rocky Mountain region suicide rate is about 17 per 100,000; the national rate is about 12 per 100,000.

3. _c_ The Mid-Atlantic states have the lowest rate at approximately 9 per 100,000 compared to the national average of 12 per 100,000.

4. _a_ In fact the following states comprise the six highest rates for all states: Wyoming, Nevada, Colorado, New Mexico, Arizona, and Montana. The rates range from 22 to 17 per 100,000; the national rate is 12 per 100,000.

5. _c_ In fact, the seven states with the lowest rates of suicide are: Rhode Island, Delaware, Massachusetts, Connecticut, New Jersey, and New York. The exception to this is Hawaii.

6. _d_ The metro-service areas with the highest rates are: Tampa-St. Petersburg, FL; Ft. Lauderdale-Hollywood, FL; and Denver-Boulder, CO, with rates of about 18 per 100,000. The national average for service areas is about 12 per 100,000.

7. _b_ The metro-service areas with the lowest rates are: New York, NY-Newark, NJ; Hartford, CT; and Boston, MA. This corresponds with the low rates for the entire Atlantic region.

8. _c_ The actual rate is 17.8 minutes. The elderly commit suicide at a rate of approximately 1 every 1 hour and 31 minutes. The young at a rate of approximately 1 every 1 hour and 43 minutes.

9. _b_ The rate is estimated at about 6-20 attempts for every suicide.

10. _a_ The rate for the elderly is 4 attempts for every suicide.

11. _d_ The rate for teenagers and college students is estimated at 200 to 1.

12. _c_ It is estimated that from 65-80% of those who commit suicide communicate or attempt to communicate their suicidal intentions to another person.

13. _c_ There are approximately 5 million living Americans who have attempted suicide. This number is growing at an estimated rate of 180,000 per year.

14. _c_ Suicide affects the lives of people outside the victim. It is estimated that at least 6 other people are affected by the suicide.

15. _c_ While the elderly make up 12% of the population, they account for 19.7% of the suicide.

Activity 6.5
TYPES OF SUICIDE

Purpose: To identify the types of suicide.

Time: 10 minutes

Background Information:

Edwin Shneidman*, in Definition of Suicide, has, after years of studying suicide, categorized suicide into six types.

Activity Procedure:

1. Match the following situations to one of Shneidman's categories.

Shneidman's Categories	Situation that Matches	Situations
1. Rational	_____	a. to thwart someone's plan
2. Reaction	_____	b. in response to a loss
3. Vengeful	_____	c. to punish someone
4. Manipulative	_____	d. to escape pain
5. Psychotic	_____	e. spontaneous decision recognized too late
6. Accidental	_____	f. to fulfill a delusion

2. Compare your responses with those provided for this activity.

Discussion and Reflection:

1. Can you list any more types? If yes, do so.

   _____

   _____

   _____

2. Do any of these types given fit into any experiences you have had. Share them if you so choose.

   _____

   _____

   _____

Answers to Item 1

1. d, 2. b, 3. c, 4. a, 5. f, 6. e

*Shneidman, E. (1985). *Definition of Suicide*. New York: John Wiley & Sons.

Activity 6.6
SUICIDE FABLES

Purpose: To differentiate between fact and fiction regarding information about suicide.

Time: 15 minutes

Activity Procedure:

1. Circle the letter T if the statement is true and circle the F if the statement is a fable. One-half of these statements are true and the other one-half are false.

SUICIDE FABLES QUESTIONNAIRE

T F 1. People who talk about suicide rarely commit suicide.

T F 2. More often than not, suicidal intentions are communicated.

T F 3. Suicidal people are fully intent on dying.

T F 4. Once a person is suicidal, they are suicidal forever.

T F 5. Even when the suicidal crisis is over, the person is still in danger.

T F 6. Suicide is no respecter of social class.

T F 7. Suicidal people aren't necessarily mentally ill.

T F 8. Men are victims of suicide more than women.

T F 9. The tendency toward suicide is inherited.

T F 10. Not all suicidal people are depressed.

T F 11. There is no correlation between suicide and alcohol use.

T F 12. If you ask someone about their suicidal intentions, you will only be encouraging them to try.

T F 13. Suicidal people frequently seek medical attention.

T F 14. Suicide is a problem basically limited to the young.

T F 15. Few professional people kill themselves.

T F 16. Suicide is as old as history.

T F 17. Women don't use guns to commit suicide.

T F 18. There is no relationship between suicide and the full moon.

T F 19. In the U.S. hot climates have the highest suicide rates.

T F 20. When someone talks about suicide, it is only an attention getting device; it is best to ignore them.

---

2. Read the facts and compare with your responses.

FACTS:

1. Most people who commit suicide give verbal or behavioral clues.

2. Suicidal intentions are communicated. The estimate is that between 65 and 80% of attempters communicate their intentions.

3. Frequently there is an ambivalence about life and death. They do not so much want to die but rather do not want to go on living in the present situation. It is in this distinction that intervention can be successful.

4. Most people who are suicidal are only so for a brief period. In fact, only about 10 to 15% of all attempters acutally kill themselves.

5. There is considered to be a period after a suicide attempt in which the person is still in danger and should have resources available.

6. Suicide cuts across all social classes.

7. People who are suicidal may indeed be very unhappy, but not necessarily mentally ill.

8. Women attempt 3 to 5 times more often than men, but men are victims 3 to 5 times more often than women.

9. While suicidal tendencies are not genetically traced, suicide appears in some families more than others.

10. Although depression is generally associated with suicide, there are many other emotions which can be linked to suicide, i.e., revenge, anger.

11. Suicide and alcohol use are strongly linked. The link is not causal yet the presence of alcohol/drugs is frequently tied to suicide.

12. Asking someone about their suicide is evidence of concern and hope. It may be the very thing that can prevent the suicide.

13. About 75% of suicidal people will visit a doctor within a month before their suicide.

14. Suicide rates increase with age and are very high for the elderly.

15. In fact, several professions have very high suicide rates, including physicians, attorneys, and dentists.

16. Reports of suicide extend back through history, including Biblical accounts.

17. Women use guns to kill themselves more than they use drugs.

18. There is no statistical relationship between increased suicides and the full moon.

19. In the USA, Arizona, New Mexico, Nevada, Florida all have high rates per 100,000. In contrast, Minnesota, North Dakota, and other northern tier states have relatively lower rates.

20. It may be true that they are asking for attention and presenting a cry for help. The worst possible thing to do would be to ignore them.

Discussion and Reflection:

1. Which statements were you surprised to find were true?

_____

_____

_____

2. Which statements were you surprised to find were false?

_____

_____

_____

3. As a class, are there other factors or fables you can add?

_____

_____

_____

4. Why do we tend to hold on to the fables in spite of evidence to the contrary?

_____

_____

_____

Activity 6.7
SUICIDE RISK TEST

Purpose: To give a simple assessment of a degree of risk when dealing with a suicidal person.

Time: 10 minutes

Activity Procedure:

1. Answer the questions in "Suicide Risk Test" for yourself so as to assess your own risk for suicide.

SUICIDE RISK TEST

Yes   No   1. There is a recent loss (job, friend, relationship, money, surgery, status, death, suicide).

Yes   No   2. Evidence of social isolation and lack of friends.

Yes   No   3. Previous suicide attempt.

Yes   No   4. Lack of philosophical or religious orientation that is opposed to suicide.

Yes   No   5. History of suicide in the family.

Yes   No   6. Over 65, bereaved or in physical pain.

Yes   No   7. Voices commanding suicide.

Yes   No   8. Depressed or coming out of depression.

Yes   No   9. A wish to die, self-destructive acts or resistance to offered help in a previous suicide attempt.

Yes   No   10. Thought of a method and have method available.

---

2. As you work with suicidal persons, consider these 10 items. Experts suggest that a person for whom an answer of yes has been given to 3 of these questions, should be considered a risk of suicide. The higher the number of yes responses, the more risk.

Discussion and Reflection:

1. If you have answered three or more "yes," you will want to talk with someone about it.

2. If you know of someone who might answer three or more "yeses," you will want to talk with them about it, or get them to talk with someone else.

3. How much does taking a test like this raise feelings of anxiety in you?

_____

_____

_____

_____

_____

Activity 6.8
SUICIDE INTERVENTION

Purpose: To provide some helpful intervention strategies.

Time: 20 minutes

Activity Procedure:

1. Circle the T for each true statement and circle the F for each false statement.

SUICIDE INTERVENTION QUESTIONNAIRE

T F 1. It is important to be positive and emphasize the most desirable options for a suicidal person.

T F 2. It is important to sound calm and understanding.

T F 3. It is important to be honest so that if the person shocks you, you show it.

T F 4. It is important to emphasize the temporary nature of the problems the person is facing.

T F 5. It is important to emphasize the moral aspects of suicide.

T F 6. It is important to stress the shock and embarrassment the suicide will cause for the person's family.

T F 7. It is important to work to establish a positive relationship with the person.

T F 8. It is important to sound confident.

T F 9. It is important to appear nonchalant.

T F 10. It is important to emphasize that the crisis will pass in time.

T F 11. It is important to minimize the person's problems.

T F 12. It is important to encourage the person to see counselors or religious advisors.

T F 13. It is important to ask questions to find out what the problem is.

T F 14. It is important to convince the person that suicide is stupid.

T F 15. It is important to talk.

T F 16. It is important to insist that the person see parents, children, counselors, or religious advisers.

T F 17. It is important to suggest that the person is crazy.

T F 18. It is important to make the person feel guilty.

T F 19. It is important to tell the person you care.

T F 20. It is important that you do not take responsibility for a completed suicide.

T F 21. It is important to talk about the person's concept of death.

T F 22. It is important not to attempt to physically take a weapon away from a suicidal person.

T F 23. It is important to argue with a suicidal person and debate the merit of suicide.

T F 24. It is important to leave the suicidal person alone after you have talked to them.

T F 25. It is important to get other people involved as soon as possible.

T F 26. It is important that you keep confidential about the person's suicidal thoughts.

T F 27. It is important to let the suicidal person know that other people have similar feelings.

T F 28. It is important to speak slowly, softly, and calmly. What you say can be less important than how you say it.

T F 29. It is important to ultimately realize that the situation is hopeless.

T F 30. It is important to find out if the person has a plan and the details of that suicidal plan.

2. Review your responses one by one and compare them with the "Suicide Intervention Do's and Don'ts.

SUICIDE INTERVENTION DO'S AND DON'TS

Answers

1. _T_   Suicidal people have reached a point of hopelessness and helplessness. They believe there are no options for their lives. Emphasizing the desirable options can serve to help the suicidal person to re-think the possibility of an option they have previously rejected.

2. _T_   You can have a calming influence on a suicidal person. Strive to stay calm and seek to understand what the suicidal person is saying.

3. _F_   Actually, this is one time where being honest might actually work against being helpful. If you are shocked, try not to show it. Appear accepting and understanding.

4. _T_   For many people, the crisis will pass if they do not kill themselves. It is important to stress that suicide is a permanent solution to a temporary situation.

5. _F_   While a person is talking about suicide is no time to enter into a philosophical debate about the morality of his or her actions. The person may feel worthless in the first place and telling him or her that what he or she is about to do is immoral may only confirm their opinion.

6. _F_   It is important to recognize that a suicidal person may be intent on embarrassing the family.

7. _T_   It may well be that the positive relationship that you establish is the only thing that will keep the person alive. Your relationship could be the proof that he or she can have a relationship and a reason to live.

8. _T_   Your confidence can be reassuring. If you are agitated and uncertain, then you probably cannot be of much help to the suicidal person.

9. _F_   No, it is more important to appear concerned and receive talk of suicide seriously. Such nonchalant approaches may work well in the movies but not in actual circumstances.

10. _T_   It is a fact that crises do pass in time. It is important to reassure the suicidal person that his or her crises can be lived with.

11. _F_   It is more important to recognize that what seems small and trivial may have brought the person to a suicidal state in the first place.

12. _T_   It is important to encourage a person to see professional people. Don't push it if the person refuses initially. Bring it up again later.

13. _T_   Asking questions is one way to keep the person engaged. It also indicates that you care enough to try to find out what the problem is.

14. _F_   No, any such attempts to make the person feel stupid, immoral, or another negative feeling may reinforce the feelings the person has about self already. It is better to be caring and understanding.

15. __T__ Yes, talk for as long as you can. The talking itself may help the crisis pass. If drugs or alcohol are involved, you can talk until the person is less under the influence and the suicidal thoughts may pass as well.

16. __F__ It is important to encourage the person; it is probably not helpful to insist.

17. __F__ This one is a joke. No, it doesn't help to tell people they are crazy!

18. __F__ See 14. Emphasizing the negative emotions during suicidal episodes is not helpful.

19. __T__ If you care, then the possibility exists that others can care as well. This may be the intervention that prevents the suicide.

20. __T__ You have to take care of yourself too. If you accept responsibility for the life of a suicidal person, you can end up hurting yourself. The task is to do the best you can and recognize that you actually have little control over whether the person lives or dies.

21. __T__ Usually, this is important. The suicidal person may not have a concept of the permanence of death. Talking about that can lead to an understanding that suicide is a permanent solution to what is a temporary problem in the person's life.

22. __T__ If you attempt to take away a gun or a knife from a suicidal person, you may be physically injured or killed. You may accidently cause the injury or death of the other person. This is a bad idea.

23. __F__ No, you may lose the argument or debate and in the process, the person.

24. __F__ No, it is important not to leave a suicidal person alone. Use the telephone to call for help or get the suicidal person to walk to another room where there are people. Don't leave the person alone.

25. __T__ Yes, the more people involved the better. It allows people to go for professional help. It divides the stress. It shows that more than one person cares.

26. __F__ No, saving a life is more important than confidentiality.

27. __T__ Sometimes suicidal people feel that they are alone. They think that their feelings and circumstances are so special that no one else has had them. If they recognize that others have the same feelings and circumstances, and have lived with them, then they might be able to live with them too.

28. __T__ Suicidal people are anxious people. You can be a calming influence on them just by being calm.

29. __F__ No, it is important to realize that no matter how bleake things can seem to a suicidal person, there are alternatives other than the drastic solution they are proposing.

30. __T__ Yes, find out the plan and see if there is anything you can do to disrupt the plan. Frequently, suicidal people have only one plan. If that one is disrupted, then they have to take time to plan another method. In that time the crisis may have passed.

Discussion and Reflection:

1. Everything considered, did you find yourself to be more of a helper or barrier to the suicidal person?

   _____

   _____

   _____

2. What do your answers to this quiz reflect about your own attitudes toward death and suicide?

   _____

   _____

   _____

3. Having completed this activity, how has your concept of a suicidal person changed? How have your attitudes about helping a suicidal person changed?

   _____

   _____

   _____

Activity 6.9
ROLE-PLAY: ASSESSING SUICIDAL RISK

Purpose: To be acquainted with and develop skills in assessing suicidal risk through role-playing.

Time: 45 minutes

Background Information:

In this activity, class members will group themselves in triads to role-play a situation. Each person of the group will have the chance to play each of the three roles. You will take turns at being a helper, client, and observer.

When you are the **helper,** you will follow the interview guidelines which will help you obtain information from your "client" regarding his or her potential for suicide. You will be asked to make a judgement as to whether your client is at low, moderate, or high risk for suicide.

As the **client,** you will have your choice of representing yourself as a low, moderate or high risk individual, using the scripts given. These scripts also will give you some ideas about what to say in portraying your role.

During your turn as **observer,** use the notes on the appropriate page to guide your observations and to serve as a framework for feedback and discussion among the triad.

Guidelines for the *Client* in Role-playing

These roles are guidelines. You may embellish them as seems appropriate. If you are asked questions about information that is not covered here, go ahead and make up responses that seem consistent with the role you are playing. The degree of risk for each of these will be noted on the reflection/discussion page at the end of this activity. For the purpose of enhancing the role-play, please do not look at the answers until all have completed their turns as client, helper, and observer.

1. Bob, age 52, divorced, two children, ages 29 and 24. Bob has recently lost his job and his future employment opportunities are not good. He has decided to kill himself. He feels isolated and without support in life. He says he is going to drive out into the countryside and shoot himself. A gun that has been his since childhood was taken from his house with bullets and placed in the car.

2. Jill, age 41, married, three children, ages 15, 13, and 10. She is thinking of suicide. Her marital problems are compounding her problems with business. So far she has been collecting pills to take and thinks she has enough now to do the job. She says that she will stay at the office after everyone leaves, take the pills, and be discovered in the morning.

3. Janet, age 19, single, no children. Janet is a college student. Her grades have been going down and she has just broken up with her boyfriend. She is thinking of suicide. She has told her roommates of her thoughts and they are concerned. She is thinking of jumping from the roof of her dorm. She knows where the key to the access door is kept. There is also a 2x4 board in her room which she says she will use to block the door when she decides to attempt.

4. Kevin, age 27, married, one child, age 2. Kevin has just lost his job and is thinking of suicide. His wife and parents are loving and supportive and are open to talking with him. He has thought of pills and maybe using his auto in the garage. The pills have not yet been acquired, but he thinks he knows where to get them. He has almost dismissed the car and garage idea since his wife is at home most of the time with the baby.

Guidelines for the *Helper* in Assessing Suicidal Risk

Read through these suggested interview questions before beginning the role-playing. When assuming the role of helper, try to maintain an attitude of concern yet directness.

1. What is happening in your life right now that brings you to talk with me?

2. Because of the problems that you are having, I feel concerned about you. I feel like I need to ask if you are thinking about suicide?

3. Is this something you have thought about before or is this the first time you have had such thoughts?

4. How long have these suicidal thoughts been on your mind?

5. Have you ever tried to take you life before?

6. Have you specifically thought about how you would take your life? Do you have a plan?

7. Tell me about your plan. Does this mean that you have the means available?

8. Did something happen that made you decide to act now?

9. Do you have somebody to talk to, any friend or member of the family that cares about how you are feeling? Is there a family doctor, therapist, or minister who could help?

10. Do you have any thoughts or plans for the future? Is there any way out of this?

Guidelines for Assessment of the Potential Suicide

The Acronyms SLAP and CARL are guidelines for your assessment of the potential suicide. Use these to help in deciding the severity of the suicide risk. Remember, all overtures to suicide are serious.

S L A P

(S) **Specificity**—how specific is the plan of action. More detail = danger.

(L) **Lethality**—the more lethal the chosen means, the greater risk.

(A) **Availability**—the easier accessibility to plans, the higher the risk.

(P) **Proximity to Help**—the more isolated the attempter is, the greater the risk.

C A R L

(C) **Chronology**—how long ago was a previous attempt. Recent = risk.

(A) **Awareness**—did the person believe the means was lethal.

(R) **Rescue**—did they help in their own rescue? Did they attempt where they could be found?

(L) **Lethality**—how lethal is the chosen method?

What level of suicidal risk did the client represent?

_____ Low   _____ Moderate   _____ High

Guidelines for *Observers* of the Role-play

Helper	Client
1. Did the helper maintain an attitude of concern, yet directness?	1. Did the client hold back information and make it unnecessarily difficult for the helper?
2. Did the helper appear calm and confident or were they uneasy in dealing with the topic?	2. Did the client make it too easy for the helper?
3. Was appropriate eye contact established and maintained?	3. Did the client remain in the role in a realistic and consistent manner?
4. Was the helper non-judgmental and accepting?	4. Other observations
5. Did the helper accurately "hear" and understand the major points of the client's circumstances.	
6. Did the helper miss some major point of clue?	
7. Other observations	

As an observer, what is your rating of the danger of suicide for the case as role-played?

_____ Low   _____ Moderate   _____ High

Activity Procedure:

1. Now, group into the triads and determine which roles to play.

2. Begin the role play. After about 7 minutes, stop and discuss what has transpired. Let the observer guide the discussion for about 5 minutes.

3. Switch roles. At the conclusion of the activity each person in the triad will have played each role.

Discussion and Reflection:

1. Was there an agreement among helper, client, and observer in assessing suicidal risk in each of the roles? Why or why not?

_____

_____

_____

2. What feelings surfaced for you in each of your roles as helper, client, and observer?

_____

_____

_____

3. For you, what stood out as being most predictive of suicidal risk?

_____

_____

_____

4. Is it really possible to assess suicidal risk? Why or why not?

_____

_____

_____

CHAPTER 7

ENCOUNTERING AIDS

7. AIDS

Our world has been assaulted by an affliction known widely as AIDS. A virus that once attacked only those in far away lands, it has become a feared killer in America. The fear of AIDS has sparked a world-wide research effort to find medical methods of countering the deadly progress of the AIDS virus.

Just as with any frightening killer, myths frequently out run facts. Many questions exist about AIDS. Most have answers. Can I get AIDS from a kiss? Can I get AIDS from an insect bite? How about a toilet seat? The answer to these questions is "No."

Can I get AIDS from sexual intercourse? Is a blood transfusion a source of AIDS? The answer to these questions is "It Depends." If you engage in what might be termed "risky sexual behavior," then the chances go up dramatically. One of the activities in this chapter help identify what is considered risky behavior and what is considered "safe sex."

What makes this chapter different from the others in this book is that it is a chapter about one form of death over which we actually do exercise control. AIDS is preventable and, therefore, death from this cause is preventable. What do we do to prevent death from AIDS? Certainly, the medical research that is being conducted right now is one source of hope. What is more certain than that research, however, is to inform ourselves about the causes of AIDS and how it is transmitted. Then, take the steps necessary to protect your life.

Activity 7.1
AIDS INVENTORY

Purpose: To promote individual and group awareness of facts about AIDS.

Time: 15 minutes

Activity Procedure:

1. Respond to the inventory provided.

AIDS INVENTORY

1. If you do not consider yourself in the "high risk" group, do you still need to be concerned about AIDS.

    Yes _____   No _____   Uncertain _____

2. The AIDS virus is spread through insect/mosquito bites.

    Yes _____   No _____   Uncertain _____

3. I am at high risk if I attend classes with someone infected with AIDS.

    Yes _____   No _____   Uncertain _____

4. Sharing drug needles is one of the most dangerous at risk behaviors.

    Yes _____   No _____   Uncertain _____

5. Heterosexuals need not be concerned about AIDS.

    Yes _____   No _____   Uncertain _____

6. Women can be less concerned about AIDS than men.

    Yes _____   No _____   Uncertain _____

7. Condoms are an effective, but not foolproof, way to prevent AIDS.

    Yes _____   No _____   Uncertain _____

8. AIDS patients have a distinctive look.

    Yes _____   No _____   Uncertain _____

9. If you think you have been exposed to the AIDS virus, you should be tested.

    Yes _____   No _____   Uncertain _____

10. People who provide help for someone with AIDS are personally at risk.

    Yes _____   No _____   Uncertain _____

---

2. When you have finished, divide into groups of five and discuss your responses.

3. Compare the responses of the group with the correct responses provided.

AIDS Inventory Responses

1. __Yes__ All people should be concerned about AIDS not only for public health reasons but because AIDS appears to be spreading from previously identified high risks groups to the population in general.

2. __No__ AIDS is primarily transmitted by sexual encounters, sharing needles and, in some cases, coming into contact with infected blood through transfusing and birth.

3. __No__ There is so little risk that it can be considered none.

4. __Yes__ The risk is very high.

5. __No__ All people need to be concerned and informed.

6. __No__ AIDS is transmitted by and to both males and females. Recent research has identified the spread of AIDS to heterosexual women.

7. __Yes__ Condoms should be used with other protection as well.

8. __No__ AIDS is undetectable by appearance. In later stages of the disease, the patient takes on an emaciated appearance.

9. __Yes__ By all means, for your sake and for the sake of any sexual partners.

10. __No__ The risk is low. With reasonable safeguards, caring for AIDS patients is not considered high risk.

Discussion and Reflection:

1. What thoughts and feelings were raised by having done this activity?

_____

_____

_____

2. Was your level of knowledge and awareness raised by this activity? Why or why not?

_____

_____

_____

3. What fears do you have about AIDS? Why do you have these fears?

_____

_____

_____

4. What specific question requires the most reflection for you?

_____

_____

_____

Activity 7.2
HIGH RISK AIDS BEHAVIORS

Purpose: To identify high and low risk behaviors related to AIDS.

Time: 10 minutes

Activity Procedure:

1. Individually place each of the behaviors listed below into one of the three categories provided.

AIDS LEVEL OF RISKS BEHAVIORS QUESTIONNAIRE

Place a check mark under L if the risk is LOW for the behavior, under AR if AT RISK by doing the behavior, and under U if the behavior is UNSAFE.

L AR U

___ ___ ___ 1. Sharing drug needless and syringes

___ ___ ___ 2. Not having sex

___ ___ ___ 3. Using same glass or utensil as an AIDS carrier

___ ___ ___ 4. Anal sex with protection

___ ___ ___ 5. Anal sex without protection

___ ___ ___ 6. Protected vaginal sex with someone who shoots drugs

___ ___ ___ 7. Unprotected vaginal sex with someone who shoots drugs

___ ___ ___ 8. Oral sex with someone who shoots drugs

___ ___ ___ 9. Protected vaginal sex with someone who engages in anal sex

___ ___ ___ 10. Unprotected vaginal sex with someone who engages in anal sex

___ ___ ___ 11. Oral sex with someone who engages in anal sex

___ ___ ___ 12. Sex with someone you don't know

___ ___ ___ 13. Sex with several partners

___ ___ ___ 14. Not shooting drugs

___ ___ ___ 15. Sex with one mutually monogamous, uninfected partner

___ ___ ___ 16. Unprotected sex with an infected partner

___ ___ ___ 17. Receiving blood

___ ___ ___ 18. Giving blood

___ ___ ___ 19. Casual contact with an AIDS carrier

___ ___ ___ 20. Mosquito/insect bite

___ ___ ___ 21. Toilet seats

___ ___ ___ 22. Using a condom

___ ___ ___ 23. Hugging

___ ___ ___ 24. Kissing

2. Divide into groups of six to tally the responses for each behavior.

3. Transfer the tally from the small groups to the chalk board for the entire class.

4. After the tally has been transferred to the chalk board, compare the class tally with the answers provided for this activity.

AIDS Level Of Risks Behavior Questionnaire Responses

1. Unsafe. Sharing drug needles is considered one of the most dangerous high risk behaviors.

2. Low.

3. Low. Such behaviors, while not recommended, are not considred at risks behaviors.

4. At Risk. Even using a condom, which is flimsy, is considered at risk behavior.

5. Unsafe. The anus is easily damaged and this is considered high risk behavior.

6. Low.

7. At Risk.

8. At Risk.

9. Low.

10. At Risk.

11. At Risk.

12. At Risk. The risk here is associated with probability.

13. At Risk. See 12.

14. Low.

15. Low.

16. Unsafe.

17. At Risk. The risk of blood transfusion has been greatly reduced with new tests.

18. Low. There is no risk in giving blood.

19. Low. There is little to no risk of AIDS in casual or even health care of AIDS victims with reasonable precautions.

20. Low. It is not apparent that insects carry the AIDS virus.

21. Low. There is no risk from this persistent myth.

22. Low. Still considered one of the best forms of prevention.

23. <u>Low.</u>

24. <u>Low.</u> There is some debate regarding lip kissing, where the risk is considered low, versus deep kissing or French kissing. In spite of this debate, the risk of contracting AIDS by kissing is considered low.

Discussion and Reflection:

1. What was your level of information for AIDS and risk?

    _____

    _____

    _____

2. What information item was most surprising to you?

    _____

    _____

    _____

3. Consider how misinformation is learned and transmitted? What misinformation did you believe? How did you learn it?

    _____

    _____

    _____

Activity 7.3
AVOIDING AIDS

Purpose: To identify the major ways in which AIDS is transmitted.

Time: 5 minutes

Background Information:

AIDS is transmitted in four major ways.

Activity Procedure:

1. In the blocks below, list what you consider are the four ways AIDS is transmitted. Each letter is the beginning of the answer.

Contracting AIDS

A
I
D
S

A	I	D	S

2. Check your responses against the answers provided at the end of this activity.

Discussion and Reflection:

1. Did you know the four ways AIDS is transmitted? Did you guess?

   _____

   _____

2. What were your misconceptions?

   _____

   _____

3. Where did your information come from?

   _____

   _____

4. How do misconceptions begin?

   _____

   _____

Answers to Activity Item 1

A = At birth
I = Intercourse, unprotected
D = Direct transfusion of untested blood
S = Sharing needles in drug use

Activity 7.4
WHO GETS AIDS?

Purpose: To familiarize one with the epidemiology of AIDS

Time: 10 minutes

Activity Procedure:

Arrange the following groups of people where AIDS cases have occurred according to their percentage of the whole on the graphic provided.

1. Sexually active homosexual and bisexual men   _____%

2. Present and past IV drug abusers   _____%

3. Persons with hemophilia   _____%

4. Persons who have had blood transfusions   _____%

5. Heterosexual contact with someone with AIDS or at risk   _____%

6. Homosexual and bisexual men who abuse IV drugs   _____%

7. Unknown or other   _____%

8. Infants born to infected mothers   _____%

AIDS Percentage of Total,
Graphically Shown by Groups of People

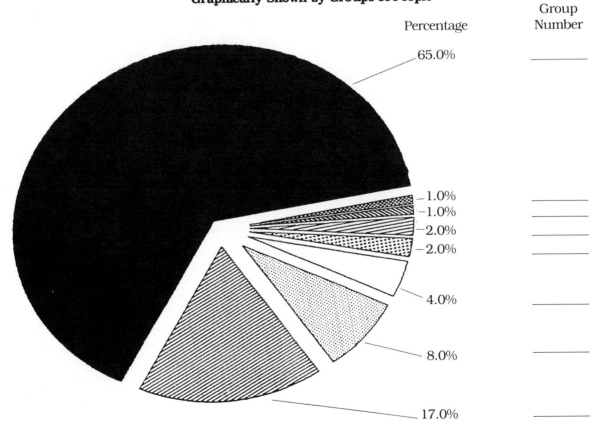

Discussion and Reflection:

1. Did any of these percentages surprise you?

2. What did you learn from these facts about how the disease is transmitted? What about blood transfusions? About birth and delivery?

_____

_____

_____

Answers According to Percentage by Group Number

1. 65%;   2. 17%;   3. 1%;   4. 2%;   5. 4%;   6. 8%;   7. 2%;   8. 1%

Activity 7.5
COMMON QUESTIONS ABOUT AIDS

Purpose: To give detailed information about AIDS.

Time: 25 minutes

Activity Procedure:

1. Answer the following questions to the best of your ability and knowledge.

COMMON QUESTIONS ABOUT AIDS

1. If somebody in the class has AIDS, are you likely to get it also?

    yes _____   no _____   uncertain _____

2. Can you become infected with AIDS from "French" kissing?

    yes _____   no _____   uncertain _____

3. Can you become infected with AIDS from oral intercourse?

    yes _____   no _____   uncertain _____

4. Using a condom during sexual intercourse will help protect you against AIDS.

    yes _____   no _____   uncertain _____

5. Your friend has anal intercourse with her boyfriend so that she won't get pregnant. She won't get AIDS from doing that, right?

    yes _____   no _____   uncertain _____

6. If you have never used IV drugs and have had sexual intercourse only with a person of the opposite sex, could you become infected with AIDS?

    yes _____   no _____   uncertain _____

7. Is is possible to become infected with AIDS by donating blood?

    yes _____   no _____   uncertain _____

8. If you had a blood transfusion three years ago, is it likely that you are infected with AIDS?

    yes _____   no _____   uncertain _____

9. Can you become infected with AIDS from a toilet seat or other objects you routinely use?

    yes _____   no _____   uncertain _____

10. Can you become infected with AIDS from a mosquito or other insects?

    yes _____   no _____   uncertain _____

---

11. As long as you are taking birth control pills, you will never get AIDS?

        yes _____   no _____   uncertain _____

12. You think you might have been infected two months ago when you had intercourse without a condom with someone you didn't know. Should you get an AIDS test?

        yes _____   no _____   uncertain _____

13. Is AIDS an upper middle class homosexual disease?

        yes _____   no _____   uncertain _____

2. Check your answers with those provided at the end of this activity.

Discussion and Reflection:

1. What myths were exposed in this test for you?

_____

_____

_____

2. What questions proved to be most sensitive to you?

_____

_____

_____

3. Did some questions stimulate more discussion than others? Which ones?

_____

_____

_____

Answers to Common Questions About AIDS

1. No	4. Yes	7. No	10. No	13. No
2. Uncertain	5. No	8. Uncertain	11. No	
3. Yes	6. Yes	9. No	12. Yes	

Activity 7.6
WHAT IS AIDS?

Purpose: To acquaint the reader with the definition of AIDS.

Time: 5 minutes

Activity Procedure:

1. Using the definitions provided below, match the definition with the term.

What is AIDS?

Term	Matching Letter	Definition
1. Acquired	____	a. body's defense system
2. Immune	____	b. a group of signs and symptoms
3. Deficiency	____	c. not born with
4. Syndrome	____	d. not working properly

---

2. The correct matches are provided at the end of the exercise.

Discussion and Reflection:

1. Does this simple definition of AIDS help your understanding of the disease?

   _____

   _____

   _____

2. What other questions do you have regarding the AIDS disease that need answers?

   _____

   _____

   _____

3. Is there any sense or relief or comfort knowing the meaning of the word AIDS?

   _____

   _____

   _____

Answers to Activity Item 1

1. c, 2. a, 3. d, 4. b

Activity 7.7
WOMEN AND AIDS

Purpose: To provide more specific information regarding AIDS and women.

Time: 15 minutes

Activity Procedure:

1. As an individual, complete the multiple choice test below.

WOMEN AND AIDS MULTIPLE CHOICE TEST

1. About _____% of all people with AIDS are women.

    a. 2
    b. 7
    c. 10
    d. 12

2. A woman is most at risk for AIDS if she has . . .

    a. shared IV needles
    b. had sex without condoms with someone who is infected
    c. both a and b
    d. none of the above

3. The _____ sex partners a woman has had, the _____ the risk.

    a. less-greater
    b. more-greater
    c. this question is irrelevant.

4. _____ can be a source of the AIDS disease.

    a. artificial insemination
    b. blood transfusion
    c. being born to a woman who is infected
    d. all of the above
    e. b and c only

5. Lesbian relationships are at a _____ risk than gay relationships for contacting AIDS.

    a. lower
    b. higher
    c. equal

---

6. If a woman has AIDS, it is known that the baby is in danger. However, what is the effect of the pregnancy on the woman's health?

    a. her health will improve
    b. her health will decline
    c. there is no affect that is attributed to AIDS

7. A woman should use a condom whenever she has _____ sex with an unfamiliar partner.

    a. oral
    b. anal
    c. vaginal
    d. b and c only
    e. a, b and c
    f. none of the above

8. The AIDS virus can be passed on to a child through . . .

    a. hugging
    b. breast feeding
    c. childbirth
    d. sharing food
    e. a, b and c
    f. b and c only
    g. none of the above

9. Of the women who have contracted AIDS, ____% have been African-American, ____% have been Latina or Hispanic, ____% have been Caucasion and 1% others.

    a. 10, 10, 79
    b. 25, 25, 49
    c. 50, 23, 26
    d. 5, 5, 89

2. Divide into groups of six to discuss the answers given by the group members. Do not look at the answers provided.

3. After discussing the group members' responses, check the answers provided at the end of this activity and discuss them in the small group.

Discussion and Reflection:

1. What facts did you discover in this multiple choice test which are different for men and women regarding AIDS?

_____

_____

_____

2. What other questions did this exam raise for you regarding AIDS and women?

_____

_____

_____

Answers to the "Women and AIDS Multiple Choice Test"

1. b   7%
2. c
3. b   more-greater
4. d
5. a   lower
6. b   the woman's health is at greater risk
7. e   during oral, anal, and vaginal sex, protection should be used
8. f   there is some possibility that AIDS can be transmitted during breastfeeding. It is, of course, well documented that AIDS is transmitted during childbirth.
9. c   50% African-American, 23% Latina, and 26% Caucasion

CHAPTER 8

ENCOUNTERING DEATH IN OUR VALUES

8. VALUES

Few would criticize the idea that the way we behave is directly tied to what we believe. Our values surely predict our behavior. While a direct correspondence may not exist between what we value and how we behave, the connection is strong enough for a consideration of values and examining them to be included in any work discussing human behavior.

In the realm of death and dying, much of what we say and do with one another comes from our values. One of the areas of our life which seems to cause us such guilt is that in the face of death our fear conquers our values. We say and do things which we do not value and, if we could recover the moment, would not say or do again. Perhaps, one way to ensure that what we value is actually practiced in the face of death is to examine those values before we ever have to test them in practice.

What do we believe about death and dying? What do I belive about life after death? What do I believe about funerals? About cremation? What do I want to say to my grandparents, my parents before they die? What do I want to say to my children before I die? What values do I want to communicate? Is killing oneself in the face of terminal disease acceptable to me? All of these questions, and others, are questions of values.

One of the most pressing questions of value we have to face in modern technological societies is what to do about the advances in technology that can extend life. So called "heroic measures" can continue biological life, even in the absence of what might be called psychological life. Is this something we wish to have happen? To ourselves? To our loved ones? How far can we extend life and still have a psychologically meaningful life? What role should medicine play in these decisions? What role should the family play? How much say should the dying person have? All? Some? None? What is the role of religion in questions of death and dying? These questions, which many view as questions of morality, have become critical as technological advances force decisions on us we have never had to face before.

The intention of this chapter is that the moral, ethical, and value decisions surrounding death and dying be encountered, examined, and discussed.

Activity 8.2
VALUES ENCOUNTER

Purpose: To respond to questions that stimulate an examination of personal values.

Time: 15 minutes

Activity Procedure:

1. Answer the multiple choice "Value Encounter Questionnaire." For some questions you may circle more than one answer.

VALUES ENCOUNTER QUESTIONNAIRE

1. What role does death play in your philosophical understanding of life?

    a. fate
    b. will of God
    c. an enemy
    d. a friend
    e. a mystery
    f. a necessity
    g. deserved
    h. other _____

2. What belief do you hold about life after death?

    a. An afterlife exists, but I don't think much about it.
    b. Life is important now and the afterlife is just a bonus.
    c. Life now is simply a prelude to the more important afterlife.
    d. No afterlife exists.
    e. I don't know.
    f. other _____

3. To whom would you like to talk shortly before death?

    a. grandparent   f. child
    b. parent   g. God
    c. brother   h. minister, rabbi, priest
    d. sister   i. famous person
    e. spouse   j. other _____

4. Would you prefer to out live your spouse?

    a. yes
    b. no
    c. I don't know.
    d. I have no opinion.
    e. other _____

5. If you had only a short time to live, how would you spend your time?

    a. I would try to put things in order.
    b. I would make no change in my life.
    c. I would become more contemplative and ponder the meaning of life.
    d. I would make a radical change in life and indulge myself (sex, drugs, gambling, travel, etc.).
    e. I would concern myself with the needs of my family.
    f. I would attempt some great feat.
    g. I would commit suicide.
    h. other _____

6. When I think about death, what I fear most is . . .

    a. the unknown.
    b. the physical corruption of my body.
    c. the pain of dying.
    d. being a burden to my family.
    e. being unable to have experiences.
    f. loss of control.
    g. unfinished business.
    h. the loss of everything and everybody I have ever known.
    i. other _____

7. How would you want to die?

    a. quietly, in my sleep
    b. quickly, but not violently
    c. quickly and violently
    d. after a significant accomplishment
    e. suicide
    f. in the line of duty
    g. saving someone else
    h. other _____

8. When would you want to die?

    a. at a young age
    b. at my prime
    c. right after the prime of life
    d. in old age
    e. other _____

9. I would be willing to die (sacrifice my life) . . .

    a. for a loved one.
    b. for a principle or a cause.
    c. for the life of a stranger.
    d. for my country.
    e. all of the above
    f. none of the above
    g. other _____

10. The meaning of death is . . .

   a. the end of everything.
   b. the end of this physical life and the beginning of another spiritual life.
   c. joining the universal, cosmic consciousness.
   d. the end of this physical life, and the beginning of another physical life as a different person, animal, or thing.
   e. I don't know.
   f. I don't care.
   g. other _____

2. Divide into small groups of 5 to discuss individual answers.

Discussion and Reflection:

1. Which of these questions provoked you the most? Why might this be so?

   _____
   _____
   _____

2. Which question provoked the most discussion in the small group? Was this a surprise?

   _____
   _____
   _____

3. What values emerged for you that you may have been only vaguely aware of?

   _____
   _____
   _____

Activity 8.3
VALUES STATEMENT

Purpose: To help identify our values about particular issues.

Time: 30 minutes

Activity Procedure:

1. Read the five areas and 23 identified issues that follow.

AREAS AND ISSUES

A. Suicide

    1. Generally _____

    2. Elderly, terminal _____

    3. Young, terminal _____

    4. Elderly, chronically ill _____

    5. Young, chronically ill _____

B. Abortion

    6. Generally _____

    7. After incest _____

    8. After rape _____

    9. Health of baby _____

    10. Health of mother _____

C. Euthanasia

    11. Active _____

    12. Passive _____

    13. Living Will _____

D. Death Options

      14. Funeral services _____

      15. Memorial services _____

      16. Burial _____

      17. Cremation _____

      18. Cryogenics _____

E. Social Issues

      19. Capital punishment _____

      20. Duty to Die _____

      22. High risks lifestyle _____

      23. Nuclear arms _____

F. Others

      24. _____

      25. _____

2. For each area, consider the issue which best reflects your own value and write in your own words in the space provided your value on that issue.

3. Respond to each of the following questions as they relate to your values in Item 2. Write "yes" or "no" for each value for each area.

QUESTIONS	A Suicide	B Abortion	C Euthanasia	D Death Options	E Social Issues	F Other
a. Are you proud of your value?						
b. Have you publicly affirmed your value?						
c. Did you choose this value after consideration of alternatives?						
d. Have you acted on this value?						
e. Have you acted consistently on this value?						

4. When finished, discuss your responses with others in the class.

Discussion and Reflection:

1. What issues provoked the greatest emotional arousal in you? Why might this have been so for you?

_____

_____

_____

2. What issues provoked the greatest emotional arousal in the class? Why might this be so?

_____

_____

_____

3. Did you find your opinion about particular issues changing as a result of class discussion? If so, what was convincing in the other's argument?

_____

_____

_____

4. What values did you feel so strongly about that no argument could convince you to change your opinion?

_____

_____

_____

Activity 8.4
VALUES QUESTIONNAIRE

Purpose: To compare personal and class answers to a regional norm group.

Time: 30 minutes

Activity Procedure:

1. Read and respond to the Values Questionnaire by placing a check mark to indicate the extent to which you agree.

    1 = Strongly Agree
    2 = Agree
    3 = No strong feelings one way or the other
    4 = Disagree
    5 = Strongly Disagree

VALUES QUESTIONNAIRE*

	SA 1	A 2	N 3	D 4	SD 5
1. If I had an illness and there was little or no hope of cure, I would want to know the truth.	____	____	____	____	____
2. If I become permanently unconscious and couldn't eat normally, I would want my life maintained with artificial feedings.	____	____	____	____	____
3. My physician has the duty to follow my wishes as a patient, even if he or she disagrees with me.	____	____	____	____	____
4. If a serious disease, known to be terminal, has caused my heart to stop beating, I would want my doctor to try to revive me.	____	____	____	____	____
5. I would want my life maintained by a breathing machine (respirator) even if there was little hope of my ever breathing on my own again. (Assuming I would remain mentally alert.)	____	____	____	____	____

Note: Permission to reprint this questionnaire has been granted by COLORADO SPEAKS OUT ON HEALTH, a project funded by The Robert Wood Foundation, Princeton, NJ; Rose Medical Center, Denver, CO; Poudre Valley, Fort Collins, CO; and St. Joseph Hospital, Denver, CO.

	SA 1	A 2	N 3	D 4	SD 5
6. Major organ transplants are a worthwhile investment of health care dollars.	____	____	____	____	____
7. There is a critical shortage of donor organs. I would support a law that assumes all suitable bodies are donors unless the next of kin refuses or the deceased left written instructions to the contrary.	____	____	____	____	____
8. Medical preparations are necessary prior to the death of an organ donor. If a dying member of my family had left no instructions, I would want to be approached before their death for permission to use their organs for transplantation.	____	____	____	____	____
9. Age is an important consideration in determining who should receive an organ transplant.	____	____	____	____	____
10. If I had a newborn infant in intensive care, I would want the doctors to do everything they could to treat it, even if the child might survive with severe handicaps.	____	____	____	____	____
11. As a parent, I would want the right to refuse treatment for my newborn infant if he or she is likely to survive with severe handicaps.	____	____	____	____	____
12. As a parent I would want the right to refuse life-sustaining treatment for my handicapped newborn infant if he or she would be a serious burden on my family.	____	____	____	____	____
13. Expensive life saving technology should be denied when a person lacks the ability to pay.	____	____	____	____	____
14. I would be willing to have taxes raised to the point where no person would be refused critical care because of inability to pay.	____	____	____	____	____
15. Expected quality of life should be a consideration when deciding whether someone is to be treated with critical care technology.	____	____	____	____	____

16. Have you heard of the "Living Will?" ____YES ____NO

17. Do you have a "Living Will?" ____YES ____NO

18. Have you heard of a "Durable Power of Attorney?" ____YES ____NO

19. Do you have a "Durable Power of Attorney?" ____YES ____NO

	SA 1	A 2	N 3	D 4	SD 5
20. A hospital that provides critical care should not be allowed to refuse treatment to a patient on the basis of inability to pay.	____	____	____	____	____
21. If a hospital becomes overwhelmed with patients who cannot pay, public funds from taxes should be made available to cover the cost of care.	____	____	____	____	____
22. All employers should be required to provide a minimum level of health insurance for their employees.	____	____	____	____	____
23. In a shortage situation, an individual who has money should be given priority over someone who does not.	____	____	____	____	____
24. I would support the decision to withdraw or withhold food and fluids from a member of my family if he or she refused them.	____	____	____	____	____
25. There are some lifesaving medical treatments that are so ordinary, usual, and basic that they should be provided by tax support to everyone, regardless of their ability to pay.	____	____	____	____	____
26. There are lifesaving treatments which are so costly, unusual, and extraordinary that they should be restricted to those people who can afford to pay.	____	____	____	____	____
27. If a family planned to institutionalize a newborn because of permanent handicaps, the financial burden upon society ought to be a consideration in deciding whether or not to undertake lifesaving treatment.	____	____	____	____	____

2. Divide into groups of six to compile responses for your group.

3. Return to entire class to compile responses for class.

4. Compare individual and class responses to norm group and the graphs shown on the pages that follow.

Discussion and Reflection:

1. As you re-read each question, reflect upon which ones caused an emotional reaction for you?

_____

_____

_____

2. Which questions caused the most controversy in class? Why might this be so?

_____

_____

_____

3. How did your personal responses compare with the norm group?

_____

_____

_____

4. How did the class response compare with the norm group?

_____

_____

_____

COLORADO RESPONSES

(No. 1) If I had an illness and there was little or no hope of cure,
I would want to know the truth.

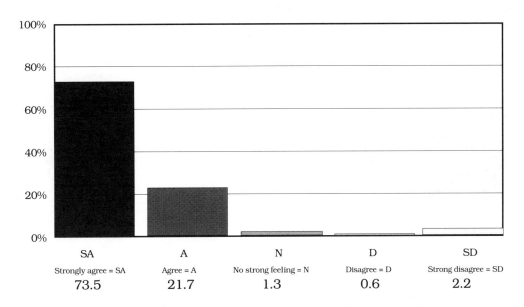

SA	A	N	D	SD
Strongly agree = SA	Agree = A	No strong feeling = N	Disagree = D	Strong disagree = SD
73.5	21.7	1.3	0.6	2.2

*"I strongly believe that a terminally ill person
should have the right to be allowed to die with dignity
rather than be kept alive and suffer."*

(No. 2) If I become permanently unconscious and couldn't eat normally,
I would want my life maintained with artificial feedings.

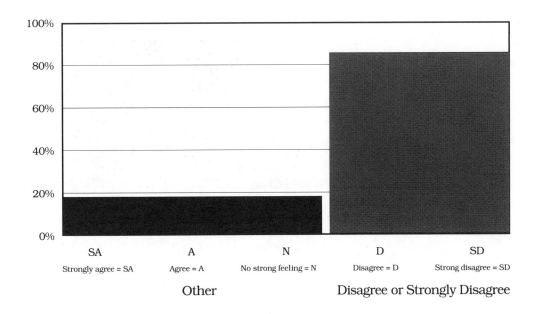

SA	A	N	D	SD
Strongly agree = SA	Agree = A	No strong feeling = N	Disagree = D	Strong disagree = SD

Other   Disagree or Strongly Disagree

(No. 3) My physician has the duty to follow my wishes as a patient,
even if he or she disagrees with me.

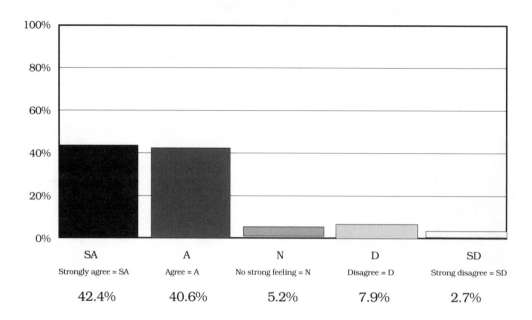

SA	A	N	D	SD
Strongly agree = SA	Agree = A	No strong feeling = N	Disagree = D	Strong disagree = SD
42.4%	40.6%	5.2%	7.9%	2.7%

"Individuals have the right to participate actively in the quality of (their) death."

(No. 4) If a serious disease, known to be terminal, has caused my heart to stop beating,
I would want my doctor to try to revive me.

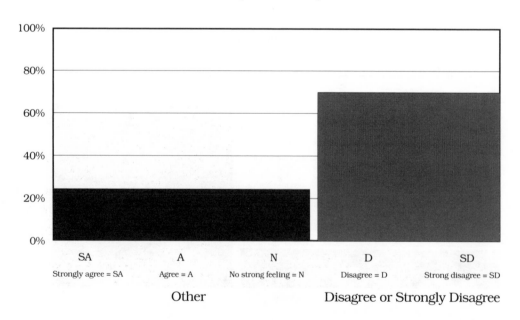

SA	A	N	D	SD
Strongly agree = SA	Agree = A	No strong feeling = N	Disagree = D	Strong disagree = SD

Other   Disagree or Strongly Disagree

(No. 5) I would want my life maintained by a breathing machine (respirator)
even if there was little hope of my ever breathing on my own again.
(Assuming I would remain mentally alert)

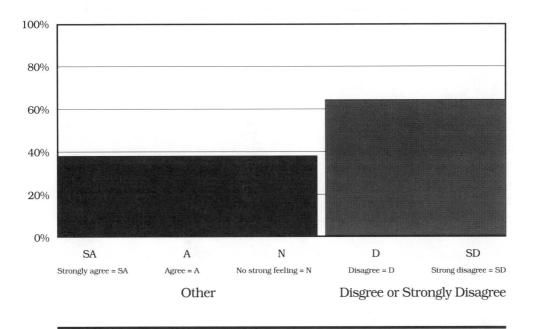

SA	A	N	D	SD
Strongly agree = SA	Agree = A	No strong feeling = N	Disagree = D	Strong disagree = SD

Other   Disgree or Strongly Disagree

(No. 6) Major organ transplants are a worthwhile investment
of health care dollars.

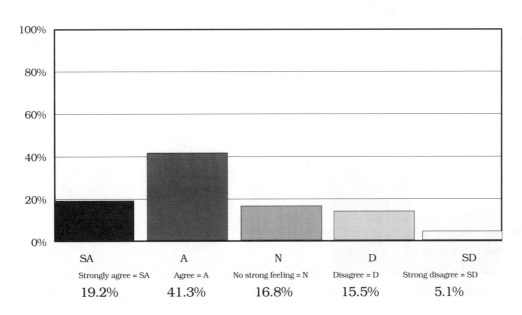

SA	A	N	D	SD
Strongly agree = SA	Agree = A	No strong feeling = N	Disagree = D	Strong disagree = SD
19.2%	41.3%	16.8%	15.5%	5.1%

"God gave us one body.
Leave the donor alone!"

(No. 7) There is a critical shortage of donor organs. I would support a law
that assumes all suitable bodies are donors, unless the next of kin refuses
or the deceased left written instructions to the contrary.

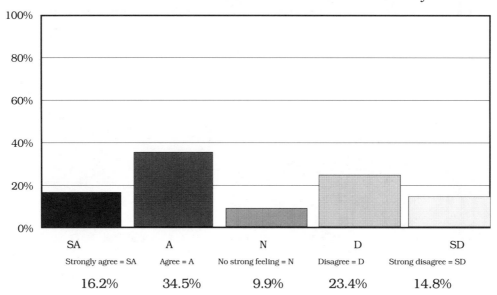

SA	A	N	D	SD
Strongly agree = SA	Agree = A	No strong feeling = N	Disagree = D	Strong disagree = SD
16.2%	34.5%	9.9%	23.4%	14.8%

"Organ donations should be mandatory"

(No. 8) If a dying member of my family had left no instructions,
I would want to be approached before their death
for permission to use their organs for transplantation.

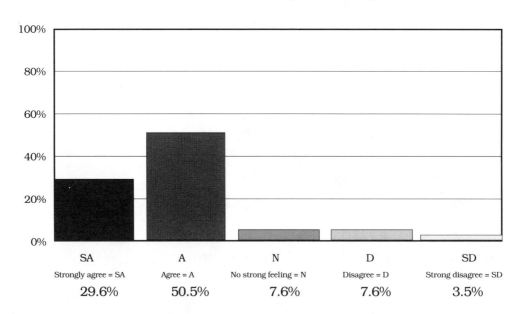

SA	A	N	D	SD
Strongly agree = SA	Agree = A	No strong feeling = N	Disagree = D	Strong disagree = SD
29.6%	50.5%	7.6%	7.6%	3.5%

"Younger people should have priority on organs.
As us older people have lived out our lives, the same privilege
should be given our young. They are our future."

**(No. 9) Age is an important consideration in determining
who should receive an organ transplant.**

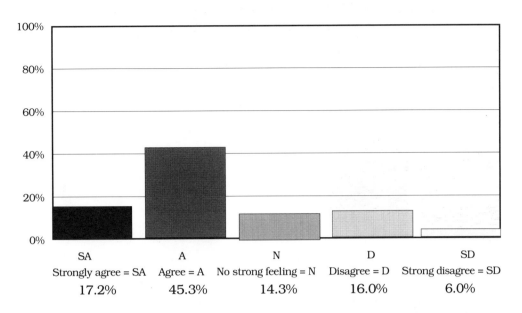

SA	A	N	D	SD
Strongly agree = SA	Agree = A	No strong feeling = N	Disagree = D	Strong disagree = SD
17.2%	45.3%	14.3%	16.0%	6.0%

*"I agree that age is an important criteria for allocating health care, but I also think
that you must look at the quality of a person's life. I would hate to see
elderly people discriminated against just because they are getting older . . ."*

**(No. 10) If I had a newborn infant in intensive care,
I would want the doctor to do everything they could to treat it,
even if the child might survive with severe handicaps.**

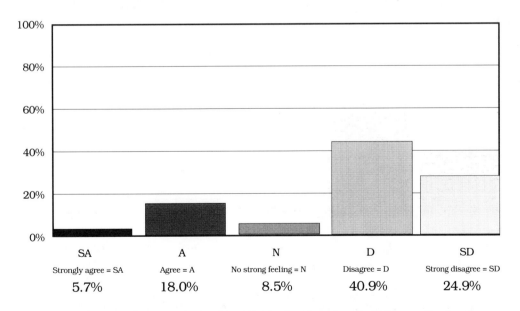

SA	A	N	D	SD
Strongly agree = SA	Agree = A	No strong feeling = N	Disagree = D	Strong disagree = SD
5.7%	18.0%	8.5%	40.9%	24.9%

*"Society does not have the right to decide who shall live on the basis
of their being a financial burden. If the life of handicapped newborn is considered to be
of no value, then what of the life of the handicapped adult, veterans and prisoners?"*

(No. 11) As a parent, I would want the right to refuse treatment for
my newborn infant if he or she is likely to survive with severe handicaps.

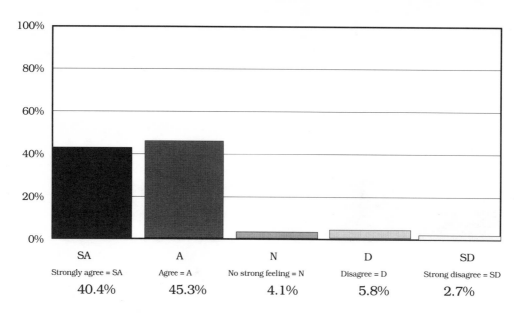

	SA	A	N	D	SD
	Strongly agree = SA	Agree = A	No strong feeling = N	Disagree = D	Strong disagree = SD
	40.4%	45.3%	4.1%	5.8%	2.7%

*"Infant's and children's decisions should be make by the parents . . .
however—Boy is this complicated!"*

(No. 12) As a parent, i would want the right to refuse treatment
for my newborn infant if he or she would be a serious burden on my family.

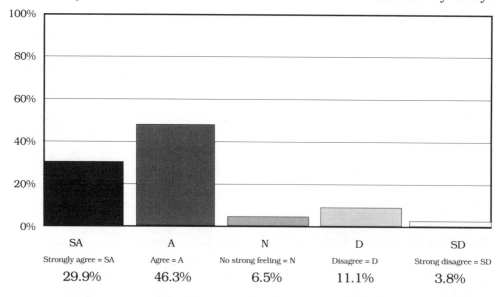

	SA	A	N	D	SD
	Strongly agree = SA	Agree = A	No strong feeling = N	Disagree = D	Strong disagree = SD
	29.9%	46.3%	6.5%	11.1%	3.8%

*"If I had known the extent of my son's damage
I would have refused treatment at birth—the option was offered,
but I didn't realize how serious my son's condition was at the time."*

(No. 13) Expensive life saving technology should be denied when a person lacks the ability to pay.

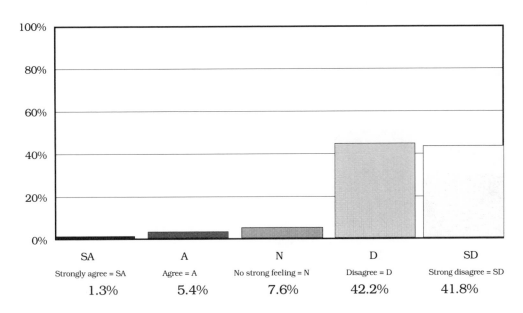

Strongly agree = SA	Agree = A	No strong feeling = N	Disagree = D	Strong disagree = SD
1.3%	5.4%	7.6%	42.2%	41.8%

"I think it's immoral for a person not to get medical care because of their income."

"Health care is not a right! Resources are limited and quality of life is important."

(No. 14) I would be willing to have taxes raised to the point where no person would be refused critical care because of inability to pay.

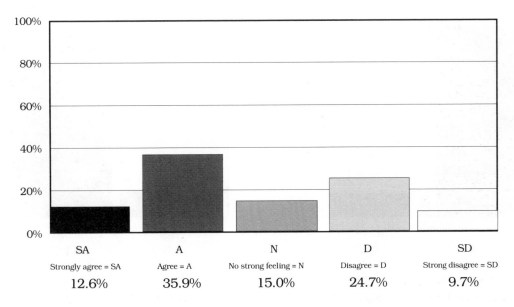

Strongly agree = SA	Agree = A	No strong feeling = N	Disagree = D	Strong disagree = SD
12.6%	35.9%	15.0%	24.7%	9.7%

I find myself saying I am not willing to pay taxes so that everyone can have equal opportunity for health care. Then I say everyone should have this equal opportunity. If I'm not willing to finance this—how can it come to be?"

(No. 15) Expected quality of life should be a consideration when deciding whether someone is to be treated with critical care technology.

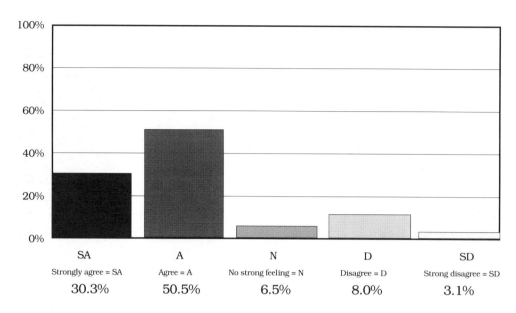

SA	A	N	D	SD
Strongly agree = SA	Agree = A	No strong feeling = N	Disagree = D	Strong disagree = SD
30.3%	50.5%	6.5%	8.0%	3.1%

"Who decides quality? What levels of quality? My 'quality of life' may differ from yours."

(No. 16) Have you heard of the "Living Will?"

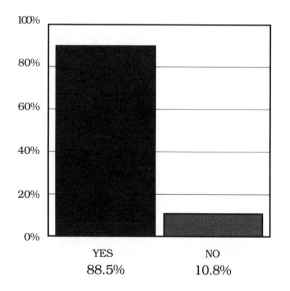

YES	NO
88.5%	10.8%

*"I believe that a living will should not be broken by **any** one."*

(No. 17) Do you have a "Living Will?"

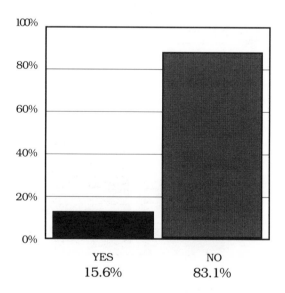

YES	NO
15.6%	83.1%

"What is the point of making a Living Will or wanting to be an organ donor if my family can override my wishes?"

(No. 18) Have you heard of a
"Durable Power of Attorney?"

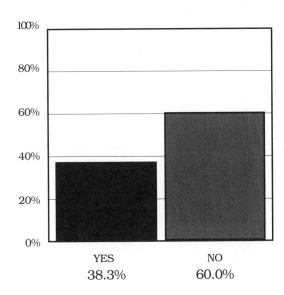

YES   NO
38.3%   60.0%

*"I believe my wishes as recorded
in writing should be honored
at the time of need."*

(No. 19) Do you have a
"Durable Power of Attorney?"

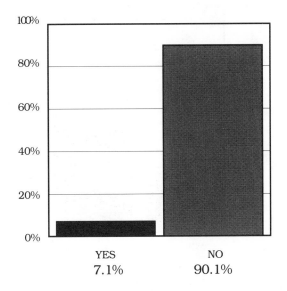

YES   NO
7.1%   90.1%

*"I think life and death circumstances
should be left to the individual,
not the family."*

(No. 20) A hospital that provides critical care should not be allowed
to refuse treatment to a patient on the basis of inability to pay.

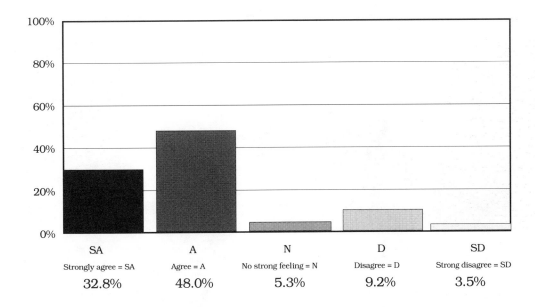

SA	A	N	D	SD
Strongly agree = SA	Agree = A	No strong feeling = N	Disagree = D	Strong disagree = SD
32.8%	48.0%	5.3%	9.2%	3.5%

(No. 21) If a hospital becomes overwhelmed with patients who cannot pay,
public funds from taxes should be made available to cover the cost of care.

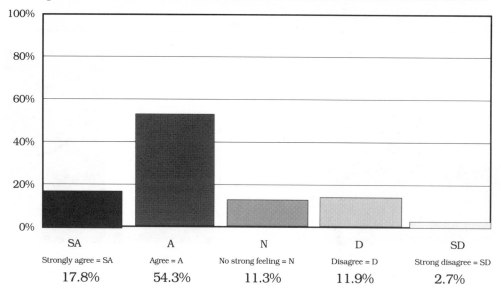

Strongly agree = SA	Agree = A	No strong feeling = N	Disagree = D	Strong disagree = SD
SA	A	N	D	SD
17.8%	54.3%	11.3%	11.9%	2.7%

*"Rather than pursuing costly transplants . . . I'd rather see the financial resources
used to assure all people basic health care, both preventative and treatment."*

---

*"Money should not be spent to prolong life if the person would be a burden.
Cost will become a greater consideration as high priced care . . . is available.
Just because it is available doesn't mean everyone is entitled to it."*

(No. 22) All employers should be required to provide a
minimum level of health insurance for their employees.

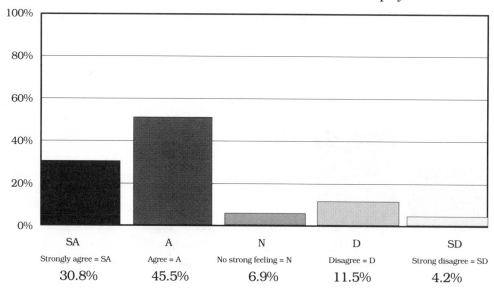

Strongly agree = SA	Agree = A	No strong feeling = N	Disagree = D	Strong disagree = SD
SA	A	N	D	SD
30.8%	45.5%	6.9%	11.5%	4.2%

*"In reality, these questions almost force one to decide whether we, as a nation,
want socialized medicine. I believe we should give basic health care to everyone,
but we cannot afford to give everyone in this country a heart transplant—
and with heart disease as the number one killer, that is the potential."*

"I think some of the toughest questions revolve around who pays."

(No. 23) In a shortage, an individual who has money
should be given priority over someone who does not.

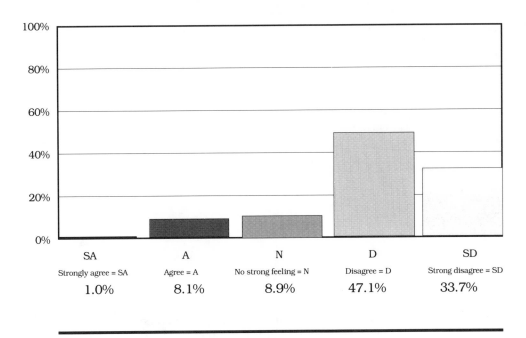

Strongly agree = SA	Agree = A	No strong feeling = N	Disagree = D	Strong disagree = SD
SA	A	N	D	SD
1.0%	8.1%	8.9%	47.1%	33.7%

(No. 24) I would support the decision to withdraw or withhold food and fluids
from a member of my family if he or she refused them.

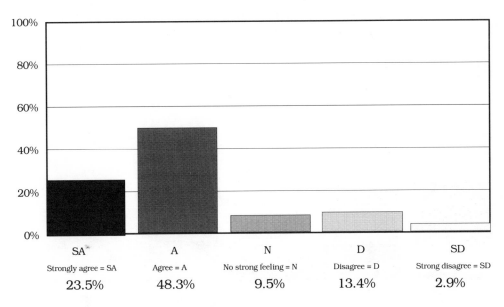

Strongly agree = SA	Agree = A	No strong feeling = N	Disagree = D	Strong disagree = SD
SA	A	N	D	SD
23.5%	48.3%	9.5%	13.4%	2.9%

"Suicide should be an acceptable means of dying for anyone who wishes (it)."

(No. 25) There are some lifesaving medical treatments so ordinary, usual and basic that they should be provided by tax support to everyone, regardless of ability to pay.

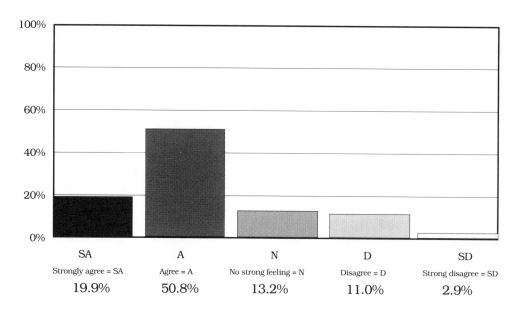

Strongly agree = SA	Agree = A	No strong feeling = N	Disagree = D	Strong disagree = SD
SA	A	N	D	SD
19.9%	50.8%	13.2%	11.0%	2.9%

*"The questions were often times very difficult to answer.
I found that by putting it away and coming back to it later,
I was able to allow sufficient time to consider things
that I had not given much thought to before.*

(No. 26) There are lifesaving treatments so costly, unusual and extraordinary that they should be restricted to those who can afford to pay.

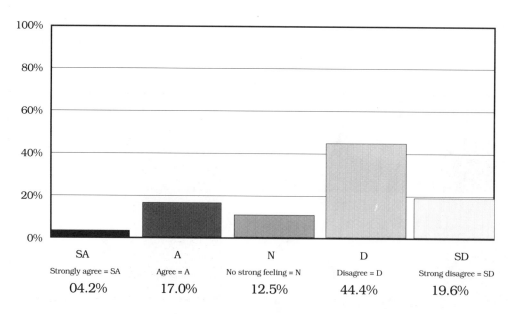

Strongly agree = SA	Agree = A	No strong feeling = N	Disagree = D	Strong disagree = SD
SA	A	N	D	SD
04.2%	17.0%	12.5%	44.4%	19.6%

*"These kinds of questions require more time and thought.
I'm glad for this opportunity to face them and to begin thinking about them."*

(No. 27) If a family planned to institutionalize a newborn because of
permanent handicaps, the financial burden on society should be
considered in deciding whether to undertake lifesaving treatment.

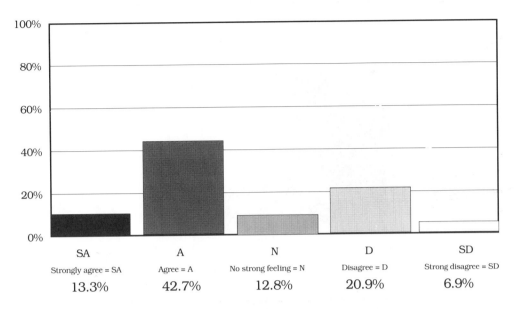

SA	A	N	D	SD
Strongly agree = SA	Agree = A	No strong feeling = N	Disagree = D	Strong disagree = SD
13.3%	42.7%	12.8%	20.9%	6.9%

"These are tough questions."

NOTE: Graphs Numbers 28 through 31 are not listed in the Values Questionnaire but
are included here for their value.

(No. 28) A "Living Will" should include
the patient's wishes either to be an
organ donor or to refuse to be
an organ donor.

(No. 29) A "Living Will" should allow
a person to decide whether to be fed
artificially or to be permitted to die,
if he or she would ever become
permanently unconscious.

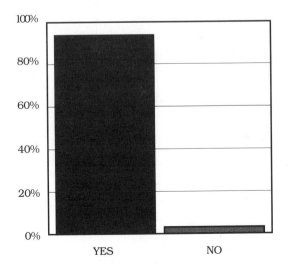

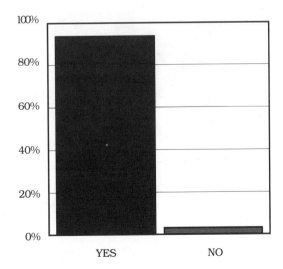

**(No. 30) A living will should include
the patient's wishes to permit
or prohibit an autopsy.**

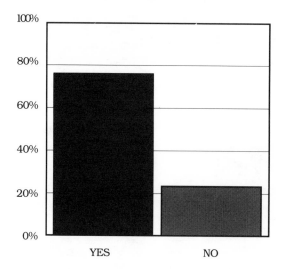

**(No. 31) I would not want members of my family to be allowed
to change my instructions concerning organ donation,
withholding foods or fluids, and autopsy instructions.**

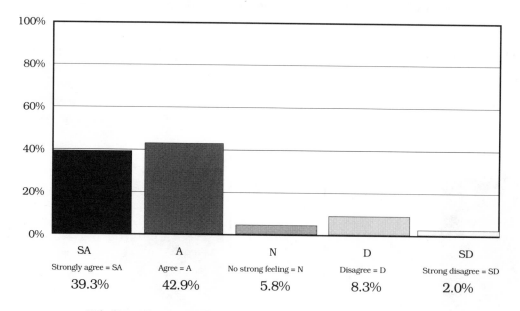

SA	A	N	D	SD
Strongly agree = SA	Agree = A	No strong feeling = N	Disagree = D	Strong disagree = SD
39.3%	42.9%	5.8%	8.3%	2.0%

*"I believe it is imperative that we, the patients, and their families,
have a choice in the kind of medical treatment we receive."*

Activity 8.5
ETHICAL DILEMMAS

Purpose: To reflect upon real ethical cases, considerations of issues and to compare how we would respond to what actually transpired.

Materials: Pen and pencil

Time: One class period

Activity Procedure:

1. Divide into groups of four or five.

2. Assign, depending upon class size, cases as follows:

   Group 1 discusses Case 1.
   Group 2 discusses Case 2—and so forth.
   Group 5 would discuss Case 1.

3. Read the cases aloud in your small group.

4. Imagine your small group is an Ethics Board. You must come up with a group statement that reflects the concerns of the Ethics Board and its decision.

5. Draw a decision from the four options listed beneath each case.

6. Present the case to the class.

ETHICAL DILEMMAS

Case 1

This is a 35 year old woman who is hospitalized with a progressive brain deterioration. She can presently respond to questions and make her wishes known. She has recently expressed a desire to die, so she has stopped eating. The hospital has reacted by force-feeding her. The woman has demanded to be permitted to die but wants drugs to ease her pain as she starves herself.

As the Hospital Administrator you decide to . . .

1. continue force feeding and provide drugs to make her comfortable.
2. discontinue force feeding and provide no drugs.
3. discontinue force feeding, provide pain diminishing drugs and agree to her wishes.
4. discontinue force feeding and provide with drugs which will cause death.

Case 2

This is a three-month-old infant who is comatose due to an accident and is on a respirator with only minimal brain activity. A slow deterioration is noted, but could have low level brain activity for a year or more. No problem exists with medical insurance or payment of hospital and doctor bills. The parents have asked that their child be removed from the respirator, which means almost certain death. The physicians and hospital have refused to go along with the parent's wishes because of the slight brain activity. One night, the father entered the room, holds the staff at gunpoint and disconnects the respirator. The father holds the child in his arms until the infant dies. After the infant dies, the father surrenders.

The action taken in this case should be . . .

1. guilty of 1st degree (premeditated) murder.
2. guilty of murder—temporarily mentally incapacitated.
3. guilty of misdemeanor, menacing.
4. no charges filed, no action taken.

Case 3

This is an elderly man, aged 73, who is diagnosed with metasticized cancer of the intestinal tract. The physicians are highly recommending surgery. Without the surgery, life expectancy is 4 to 6 months. With the surgery, life expectancy is estimated at 1 to 2 years. All of this is explained by the physicians with their recommendation and understood by the patient. The patient has already signed the necessary papers consenting to the surgery. The morning of the surgery, the nurses find the patient anxious about the surgery and expressing some fear of dying. The experienced nurses attribute this to normal anxiety and prepare the patient. As they wheel the patient to the operating room, he again voices his anxiety and fear of dying during the operation.

As the supervising nurse you . . .

1. continue with surgery as planned—reassuring and calming the patient as you go into the operating room.
2. have the person verbally re-commit to the surgery.
3. have the person sign another consent form.
4. postpone the surgery.

Case 4

The seven-year-old son of an unemployed, uninsured single parent, is diagnosed with leukemia. The physicians recommend that the boy receive a bone marrow transplant. Applying through Medicaid, the mother was assured that funds for the operation would be available, and the necessary arrangements with the hospital were initiated. However, the state legislature shortly thereafter votes to cut Medicaid funding for heart, liver, pancreas and bone marrow transplants.

The hospital should . . .

1. demand $100,000 in advance before performing the transplant.
2. require $100,000 deposit and assist in fund raising efforts.
3. hospital seeks to identify another facility in a neighboring state where the operation can be performed under present circumstances.
4. hospital and physicians donate facilities and services.

Discussion and Reflection:

1. How different were your choices from the real outcomes which are provided at the end of this activity?

_____

_____

_____

2. How different were other responses in the class?

_____

_____

_____

3. What feelings and emotions were apparent as you read and made decisions about each of the cases?

_____

_____

_____

Ethical Dilemmas: Outcomes of the Four Cases

Case 1—A similar case was resolved for the hospital when the patient was released to her home, therefore alleviating the hospital of any responsibility.

Another similar case in Colorado had to be referred to the courts. The patient was allowed to refuse force feeding and subsequently died.

Case 2—The man was not charged with murder or manslaughter but was charged with a misdemeanor. About one month later he was under psychological care due to a suicide attempt.

Case 3—The man died of complications during the surgery.

Case 4—The hospital demanded $100,000 in advance. Friends and relatives started a public fund-raising campaign that drew much media attention. However, the boy died before sufficient funds could be raised.

Activity 8.6
MORAL DILEMMA

Purpose: To explore the problems associated with decisions about one's own death due to illness and disease.

Time: 15 minutes

Activity Procedure:

1. Read the "Moral Dilemma" below.

2. Select or prepare a decision to the dilemma.

3. Divide into small groups of 4 or 5 to discuss your decision.

4. After each person has presented a decision and discussed reasons for decisions, reevaluate your decision, and reaffirm it or make a different decision.

MORAL DILEMMA

You are a woman, 38 years old, married, and a mother of three young children (10, 8, 6). You have received a diagnosis of cancer from your physician and have been given a prognosis of about one year to live. Hope for remission is unrealistic.

During the time of your dying you will have to be hospitalized, will have to undergo a variety of operations, and will need other therapies to maximize your dwindling life expectancy. Sooner or later you will lapse into a coma and need to be placed on several life-sustaining machines. Your body will swiftly deteriorate. Pain will become very severe and you will be given heavier and heavier dosages of anti-pain drugs.

Your options . . .

a. I will stay alive until death takes me, will be appreciative of all the efforts that have been and will be made on my behalf to extend my life and make my dying easier.

b. I will request family and physician to permit me to die with dignity when only "heroic measures" will keep me alive.

c. When the dying process becomes unbearable, I will administer a lethal dose of drugs and end my own life on my own terms.

d. Should I not be able to act on my own behalf to take my own life, I will have arranged with my physician and/or family to act for me to achieve an early death.

e. Other

Discussion and Reflection:

1. In making your personal decision what did you consider in your decision?

   _____

   _____

   _____

2. When you heard the arguments of others, did you question your own decision?

   _____

   _____

   _____

3. Consider for a moment, in the small group, where did our values about this decision come from?

   _____

   _____

   _____

Activity 8.7
NEAR DEATH EXPERIENCE (NDE) QUIZ

Purpose: To understand what a near death experience is.

Time: 15 minutes

Activity Procedure:

1. Complete the "Near Death Experience (NDE) Quiz."

NEAR DEATH EXPERIENCE (NDE) QUIZ

Answer the following, true or false. Circle your response.

T   F   1. The length of resuscitation effort correlates positively with the frequency of report of NDE.

T   F   2. Less than 30% of those critically ill or injured persons who are revived report having had an NDE.

The following could be characteristics of a primary NDE. Circle them true or false.

T   F   3. Sense of security and well-being.

T   F   4. Feeling of warmth.

T   F   5. Subsequent increase in fear of dying.

T   F   6. Presence of relatives or friends in the NDE.

T   F   7. Heightened sense of fear and depression.

T   F   8. The NDE tends to diminish sense of purpose and direction in life.

T   F   9. A light or being of light is encountered.

T   F 10. Sensation of rising or floating.

T   F 11. A life review takes place.

T   F 12. A buzzing or humming high pitched tone is heard.

T   F 13. A sense of journeying or moving through a tunnel is experienced.

T   F 14. A choice point of continuing or turning back is reached.

T   F 15. Typically the presence of two companions is reported.

Other questions:

T   F 16. It has been shown that age, gender, socio-economic status and the nature of the life threatening condition all influence the frequency of NDE.

T   F 17. All NDE's are experienced as positive.

---

2. Group into subgroups of 4 or 5 to share views of items in the NDE Quiz.

3. Compare answers to those provided at the end of this activity.

Discussion and Reflection:

1. If you know of a person who has reported an NDE share it. Compare their report to what was learned in this activity.

_____

_____

_____

2. Why is interest in NDE a recent phenomena?

_____

_____

_____

3. Do you think that NDE is proof of an after life?

_____

_____

_____

Answers to Near Death Experience (NDE) Quiz

1. F	5. F	9. T	13. T
2. T	6. T	10. T	14. T
3. T	7. F	11. T	15. F
4. T	8. F	12. T	16. F
			17. F

Activity 8.8
AFTERLIFE

Purpose: To reflect upon your beliefs about an afterlife.

Time: 20 minutes

Activity Procedure:

1. Complete the "Afterlife Questionnaire."

AFTERLIFE QUESTIONNAIRE

1. I believe in some form of life after death.   Yes _____   No _____

2. The probability that my answer is correct is . . .

    100% _____   75% _____   50% _____   25% _____   0% _____

3. Many different concepts of life after death (heaven, reincarnation, cosmic consciousness, etc.) exist. In the space below, describe your concept of an afterlife. If you don't believe in an afterlife, describe your belief.

    _____

    _____

    _____

    _____

    _____

4. Suppose you want to persuade someone that there is no afterlife. What evidence would you use?

    _____

    _____

    _____

    _____

    _____

5. Suppose you want to persuade someone that there is an afterlife. What evidence would you use?

    _____

    _____

    _____

    _____

    _____

---

6. What is the best thing about an afterlife? The worst thing?

_____

_____

_____

_____

_____

7. How did you come to your present belief?

_____

_____

_____

_____

_____

2. Group into subgroups of 4 or 5 each and share responses and reasons for each.

3. Summarize the various responses in terms of values held.

Discussion and Reflection:

1. Which responses reflected traditional beliefs as espoused by various religions?

_____

_____

_____

2. How difficult was it to share some of this? Are some of our views too private for sharing? Why?

_____

_____

_____

CHAPTER 9

ENCOUNTERING DEATH AS OUR HELPER

9. HELPING

Dying is a time when people we know need help. They need help with the ordinary tasks of life. They need emotional support. Someone once said that a task shared is a task halved. That is a way of helping. By helping, we do something to lighten the load. We cannot take the problem away, but we can make it more bearable.

Part of the problem of helping during a time of dying is that our behavior may not match our intention. We may be well motivated and yet say or do something that is not helpful? How can we tell the difference? What is helpful and what is not? Is there a right thing to say? Activities in this chapter address these questions and are aimed at helping the reader be of more, and better, help to someone who is dying or who is a survivor of a death.

Helping someone with the tasks that surround a death is important. For example, the daily tasks of life continue even though a family is grieving. Food must be prepared, the yard must be maintained, cards sent and responded to, utility bills still must be paid. People may need transportation. Relatives may need transportation from the airport. Errands are to be run. The children may be in school. Lunches might need to be prepared. In all of these, friends and neighbors can be of help.

Helping another emotionally depends on surprisingly few variables.

First, one must care enough to want to be of help.

Second, the willingness must exist to spend the time necessary to be of help.

Third, also a willingness must exist to listen.

Fourth, one must have the capacity to be non-judgemental.

Without being elaborate, we have provided a definition of helping. Once a person who wants to be of help moves beyond these four guidelines, then the danger exists that they are no longer being helpful. When we do something other than the four principles above, then one may be judgemental, moralistic, advise giving, discounting, humoring, or even condemning. Obviously, none of these things can be construed as helpful. Imagine, if you will, how you would feel if after the death of someone you loved, your friends said to you such things as, "You need to handle your grief better," or "It's better that things happened this way," or "Just get back to work so you don't have to think about it," or "You're strong. You'll get over it," or "Boy, when they say the good die young, they sure were wrong about your granddad," or "I thought you would be over this by now." Obviously, none of these comments are helpful. Seen nakedly, they are obvious. The problem is often that such comments are subtle and hard to detect. Use activities in this section to better understand what is considered helpful and why, what is not helpful and why not.

One final note. The authors do not consider helping to be the sole province of professionals. While professionals can be, and often are, helpful to grieving people that does not mean that people who are not professional helpers cannot also be of help. Using activities in this chapter can assist the reader in learning how to be of help and comfort to dying people and survivors.

Activity 9.1
STAGES OF DYING

Purpose: To identify the stages of dying, understand their fluid application, and develop appropriate responses.

Time: 30 minutes

Background Information:

Elizabeth Kubler-Ross identified five stages of dying that aid us as helpers in understanding the feelings of the dying. These stages apply to a lingering death, where time and thought allow for a processing of feelings. Some critique of Kubler-Ross points to these stages as not chronological or mandatory. People respond in various ways to their own impending death; with their own time line. Not all people experience all of these stages. Finally these stages do not necessarily apply to the grief processes of survivors.

Nevertheless, a helpful procedure is to have a glimpse of the stages, and to see how they can help us be effective caretakers of the dying.

KUBLER-ROSS STAGES	CHARACTERISTICS
Denial	No, not me!
Anger	Why me?
Bargaining	Yes me, but . . .
Depression	Yes me. Poor me!
Acceptance	Yes, me.

Activity Procedure:

1. Identify in column two the stage for each statement in the first column that may be made by one who is dying.

2. Read the typical response in column three.

3. Give in column four an alternative response that is more helpful than the stereotypical one.

STATEMENT	STAGE	TYPICAL RESPONSE	IDEAL RESPONSE
These damn doctors don't know the pain I'm in. They don't know what the hell they're doing.		Oh, I'm sure they are doing the best they can. Trust your doctor.	
I'm getting up out of this hospital. I've got things to do.		Stay and rest so you can get better. Then you can come home.	
I just want one more Christmas with my family.		Don't worry, you'll probably out live us all.	
I am ready to go.		Oh, don't say that.	
(Silence, turning away, weeping)		You're just making this harder on yourself and us.	

4. Group into subgroups of 4 or 5, compare responses and discuss which would be more helpful. Remember to be helpful and constructive about each other's responses.

Discussion and Reflection:

1. What makes the "typical" responses unhelpful?

_____

_____

_____

2. Were you, as an individual, and/or class, able to construct more helpful responses?

_____

_____

_____

Activity 9.2
THE TASKS OF MOURNING

Purpose: To understand the tasks of mourning and how by understanding those tasks we can aid in helping a survivor.

Time: 20 minutes

Activity Procedure:

1. Recall a significant death of a grandparent, parent, child, spouse, or friend. (If you haven't had a significant death close to you, choose one and speculate.)

2. Write the tasks, phases, and periods of adjustments you have gone through (or will) in the grieving process. You may list activities, tasks, comments, or processes you would undergo in adjusting to this death.

_____
_____
_____
_____
_____
_____

3. Use your list from Item 2 and categorize your comments under the *Four Tasks of Mourning* according to J. W. Worden.*

   a. ACCEPTING THE REALITY OF THE LOSS

   _____
   _____
   _____
   _____
   _____
   _____

   b. EXPERIENCING THE PAIN OF THE DEATH

   _____
   _____
   _____
   _____
   _____

---

*Worden, J. W. (1982). *Grief counseling and grief therapy*. New York: Springer Publishing Company.

c. ADJUSTING TO THE ENVIRONMENT WHERE THE DECEASED IS MISSING

_____
_____
_____
_____
_____
_____

d. WITHDRAWING EMOTIONAL ENERGY AND RE-INVESTING IT IN ANOTHER RELATIONSHIP

_____
_____
_____
_____
_____
_____

4. Group into subgroups of 4 or 5 to share responses and why your responses were placed as they were.

Discussion and Reflection:

1. Which of Worden's tasks ended up with the longest list?

_____
_____
_____

2. Which is the most difficult task?

_____
_____
_____

3. Which is the easiest task?

_____
_____
_____

4. Compare results between those who have experienced a significant death with those who have not. What do you see?

_____
_____
_____

Activity 9.3
THE LANGUAGE OF SYMPATHY AND EMPATHY

Purpose: To distinguish between helpful and not helpful expressions of concern.

Time: 20 minutes

Activity Procedure:

1. Write in the spaces provided those phrases or comments you have heard said either to you or another person concerning a death. Categorize them as to whether they were helpful, not helpful, or neutral.

    a. HELPFUL VERBAL EXPRESSIONS OF SORROW AND CARING

        Example: "I was saddened to hear about the death of . . ."

        _____

        _____

        _____

        _____

    b. NOT HELPFUL EXPRESSIONS
        Example: "It was for the best."

        _____

        _____

        _____

        _____

    c. EXPRESSIONS WHICH ARE NEUTRAL OR AMBIGUOUS

        _____

        _____

        _____

        _____

2. In small groups, add to each other's list.

Discussion and Reflection:

1. What caused your answers to fall under each category?

   _____

   _____

   _____

2. What feeling do each of those phrases elicit for you?

   _____

   _____

   _____

3. What differences did you find among other classmates?

   _____

   _____

   _____

Activity 9.4
CLICHES

Purpose: To unmask cliches that are not helpful.

Time: 15 minutes

Background Information:

Some of the more familiar cliches used to "help" grieving people feel better are often harmful rather than helpful. The intent may be good, but sometimes our words are woefully inadequate.

Activity Procedure:

1. For each cliche, identify what is wrong about it, and then give what you think would be a better response.

   a. (Cliche) "You must be strong for your children."

      (What's wrong) _____

      _____

      _____

      (Better response) _____

      _____

      _____

   b. (Cliche) "You've got to get a hold of yourself."

      (What's wrong) _____

      _____

      _____

      (Better response) _____

      _____

      _____

   c. (Cliche) "No sense in dwelling on the past."

      (What's wrong) _____

      _____

      _____

      (Better response) _____

      _____

      _____

d.   (Cliche) "You (they) should be over this by now."

(What's wrong) _____

_____

_____

(Better response)   _____

_____

_____

e.   (Cliche) "It was for the best."

(What's wrong)   _____

_____

_____

(Better response)   _____

_____

_____

f.   (Cliche) "It was God's will."

(What's wrong)   _____

_____

_____

(Better response)   _____

_____

_____

g.   (Cliche) "I know just how you feel."

(What's wrong)   _____

_____

_____

(Better response)   _____

_____

_____

h.   (Cliche) "If there is anything I can do, call me."

(What's wrong)   _____

_____

_____

(Better response)   _____

_____

_____

i. (Cliche) "Their time had come."

    (What's wrong)   _____

    _____

    _____

    (Better response)   _____

    _____

    _____

j. (Cliche) "Don't worry, the children won't remember."

    (What's wrong)   _____

    _____

    _____

    (Better response)   _____

    _____

    _____

2. Assemble in groups of 5 or 6 people.

3. Read and share your Better Responses with one another.

4. Choose one to report and explain to the rest of the class how it is better.

Discussion and Reflection:

1. Have you personally heard any of the cliches in Procedure 1? Can you recall how you felt when you heard it?

_____

_____

_____

2. Perhaps a more risky question is . . . have you spoken any of the cliches? Can you remember your feelings as you spoke it? What were the reactions of the people to whom you spoke?

_____

_____

_____

3. What is the purpose of stereotype, cliche responses?

_____

_____

_____

Activity 9.5
TALKING ABOUT DEATH

Purpose: To understand how you would communicate about death.

Time: 15 minutes

Activity Procedure:

1. Create in words a situation in which you might have to break the news to a close friend that some very close to the friend has died. Give background and context.

_____
_____
_____
_____
_____
_____
_____
_____
_____
_____
_____
_____
_____
_____

2. Write what you would say to your close friend.

_____
_____
_____
_____
_____
_____
_____
_____
_____
_____
_____
_____
_____
_____

3. Identify some of the friend's anticipated reactions and how you would respond to them.

_____

_____

_____

_____

_____

_____

_____

_____

_____

_____

_____

_____

_____

_____

Discussion and Reflection:

1. Describe to the members of your group any discomfort you felt in this task.

_____

_____

_____

2. What fears did you encounter as you thought about telling someone about a death?

_____

_____

_____

3. What was helpful to you in doing this activity?

_____

_____

_____

Activity 9.6
NO ONE IS AN ISLAND

Purpose: To identify one's support system.

Time: 20 minutes

Activity Procedure:

1. In your experience with yourself, friends, and relatives who have encountered a death, identify to what extent were resource people or media sought for help and emotional support. Circle the extent by each of the resources suggested.

N = None	S = Some	H = Helpful		VH = Very Helpful			
RESOURCE	**EXTENT OF HELPFULNESS**			**CLASS TOTAL**			
friend	N	S	H	VH	N ___ S ___ H ___ VH ___		
minister	N	S	H	VH	N ___ S ___ H ___ VH ___		
professional counselor	N	S	H	VH	N ___ S ___ H ___ VH ___		
relative	N	S	H	VH	N ___ S ___ H ___ VH ___		
books	N	S	H	VH	N ___ S ___ H ___ VH ___		
pamphlets	N	S	H	VH	N ___ S ___ H ___ VH ___		
films/TV/video	N	S	H	VH	N ___ S ___ H ___ VH ___		
other (specify)							
_____	N	S	H	VH	N ___ S ___ H ___ VH ___		
_____	N	S	H	VH	N ___ S ___ H ___ VH ___		

2. After you have finished Procedure 1, tally the total for each resource for the class.

Discussion and Reflection:

1. Identify patterns and understandings that you can glean from having completed procedures 1 and 2.

   _____

   _____

   _____

2. Summarize why you think certain things or persons were chosen?

   _____

   _____

   _____

3. Based on your experience and comments by others, summarize which resources are part of one's best support system.

   _____

   _____

   _____

Activity 9.7
GRIEF WORK: LETTER WRITING

Purpose: To confront unspoken feelings about a person who has died.

Time: 30 minutes

Background Information:

The following task is risky and powerful. Recognize that and recognize your support people if you should need them.

Activity Procedure:

Write a letter to a person close to you (this could be someone who has died or is dying, or someone special with whom you want to share these thoughts). We will give you a start, you complete the sections of the letter.

LETTER

Dear _____

    I am in a class that is about death and dying. We have talked about our fears and hopes as we have encountered death on a personal level. What I have learned is . . .

    What I want to say to you personally now is..

Discussion and Reflection:

1. Will you send this letter if possible? Why or why not?

   _____

   _____

   _____

2. Will you share this letter with anyone? If so, with whom?

   _____

   _____

   _____

3. Did vague and undifferentiated values begin to take form as you wrote the letter?

   _____

   _____

   _____

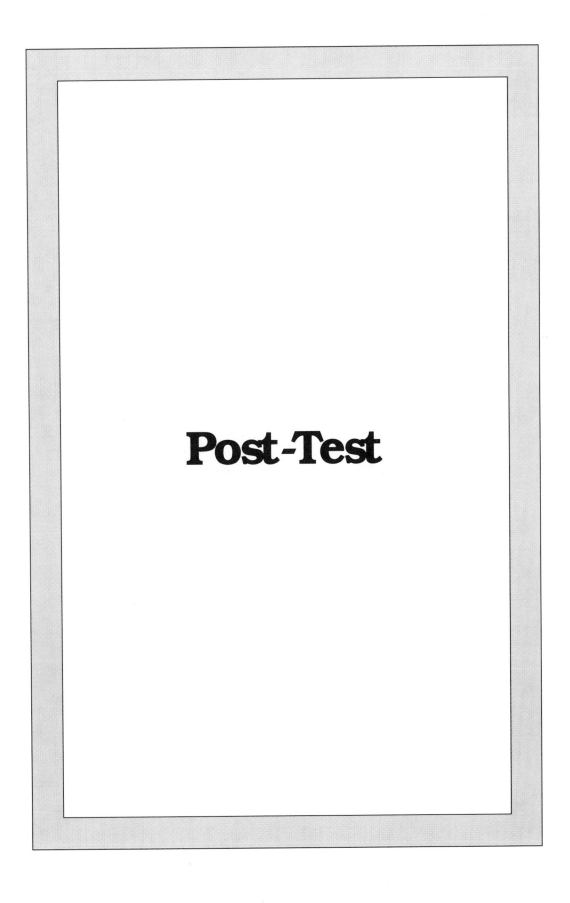

Post-Test

ENCOUNTERING DEATH SCALE:
POST-TEST

Purpose: To compare the pre-test scores with post-test scores to determine the effects of the class on one's perceived ability to cope with death.

Time: 40 minutes

Activity Procedure:

1. Respond to each question on the 5 point scale from "strongly agree" to "strongly disagree".

2. Respond independently to each item.

3. Compare your pre-test score with your post-test score to determine personal changes.

4. When all members of the group have completed the "Encountering Death Scale," sum the class response to each question to determine a class average for each question.

5. Compare pre-test and post-test class responses to determine overall class changes.

ENCOUNTERING DEATH SCALE

Directions: Please indicate your response to each of the statements using the following scale:

Strongly Disagree	Disagree	Neutral	Agree	Strongly Agree
1	2	3	4	5

_____ 1. I am at ease in thinking about death.

_____ 2. It is important to discuss death and death related topics.

_____ 3. I am prepared to face my own death.

_____ 4. I can be helpful in assisting others to face death.

_____ 5. I can help someone who is feeling suicidal.

_____ 6. I can talk about death with others.

_____ 7. I understand the role of many of society's institutions (hospital, funeral home, nursing home, etc.) in dealing with death.

_____ 8. Sudden death is very frightening to me.

_____ 9. I understand my fears about death.

_____ 10. I understand my culture's response to death.

_____ 11. I can talk with a dying person.

_____ 12. I can share my thoughts and feelings about death with my family members.

_____ 13. I understand how AIDS is transmitted.

_____ 14. I can assess the seriousness of suicide threat.

_____ 15. I can help others who have faced death in a natural disaster.

_____ 16. I can help someone deal with the death of a pet.

_____ 17. I can assist others who are grieving a death.

_____ 18. I understand the ethical problems that accompany prolonged terminal illness.

_____ 19. I can plan a funeral.

_____ 20. I can help my family members deal with death.

Discussion and Reflection:

1. Individually, note the questions on which you see the greatest change. In what direction did they change? What accounts for this change?

   _____

   _____

   _____

   _____

2. As a class, in what areas did you notice the greatest changes? What might account for this change?

   _____

   _____

   _____

   _____

3. What areas not covered by this inventory were important to you as you experienced this death and dying class?

   _____

   _____

   _____

   _____

ALPHABETICAL INDEX OF ACTIVITIES

A

B

C

D

E

F

G

H

I

L

M

N

P

R

S

T

V

W

Y

TOPICAL INDEX

Topic   **Activity Number**

A

Accidental Death 5.4
Afterlife 8.7, 8.8
Aging 1.9
AIDS 7.1, 7.2, 7.3, 7.4,
                                                                                 7.5, 7.6, 7.7
      avoiding 7.3
      definition 7.6
      epidemiology 7.4
      inventory 7.1
      questions 7.5
      risk 7.2
      transmission 7.3
      women 7.7
Anecdotes 3.4
Art 3.11, 3.16
Attitudes
      general 2.4
      history 3.11
      teaching 2.4
      toward death and dying 1.6
      toward suicide 6.1

B

Brother, death of 2.8

C

Care, dying 4.3
Case studies 8.5, 8.6
Cause of death 5.6
Childhood
      friends, death of 2.6
      games, songs, rhymes 2.7
      understanding of death 2.5
Christmas 3.14
Church 4.4
Cliches 9.4
Coat of arms 8.1

T

U

V

W

ABOUT
THE
AUTHORS

Ira David Welch, Ed.D., is a professor and Director of Training of counseling psychology at the University of Northern Colorado. He is a licensed psychologist and has a private practice in Greeley, Colorado. Dr. Welch has published a number of books in the fields of education and psychology as well as many professional articles.

Dave, as he is called by nearly everybody, is married to Marie. In their over 25 years of married life, the two best things they have ever done is to created David, now 19 and in college, and Daniel, now 15. David and Dan are both dedicated soccer players and Dave is a soccer referee. Marie is a teacher, an actress, and a mountain climber. Marie has hiked to the peak of more than 25 of Colorado's fourteen thousand foot mountains. The family unit is completed by Frisker the Dog who has somehow managed to worm his way into each of their hearts.

Richard F. Zawistoski has a B.A. in Psychology from Towson State University and a Masters of Divinity from Luther-Northwestern Theological Seminary, St. Paul, Minnesota. He is an ordained paster of the Evangelical Lutheran Church of American, since 1973, where he has served both as parish pastor and campus pastor.

While at the University of Northern Colorado, from 1982-1989, Richard taught classes in death and dying and in Human Values. Previous commitments have include Hospice Board, the North Colorado Medical Center Ethics Board, and resource trainer for "helpline."

Richard presently serves as the Lutheran Campus Pastor at Indiana University, Bloomington, Indiana. He now leads grief support groups on the campus and is a member of the Resident Hall Resource Team at the University. Various workshops, Resident Assistant training consultation, and Quad wide programs are offered the student and leaders at IU.

Recently at a gathering of over 2,000 college students, in Louisville, Kentucky, Richard conducted three workshops on "When Someone Dies . . . Understanding Grief." He is available especially to church groups, to conduct workshops and consult in the area of theology and grief related issues.

David Smart has a Ph.D. in Psychology from the University of Utah and is presently the director of the University Counseling Center at the University of Northern Colorado. He holds the rank of professor in the Department of College Student Personnel Administration. He teaches courses in death and dying, suicidology, and crisis intervention at both the graduate and undergraduate levels. These university courses have been taught both on campus and at locations across a seven-state region of the Western United States. He is a consultant and trainer to numerous nursing homes, hospices, churches, and care programs which deal with grief, loss, and death. In addition, Dr. Smart consults with law enforcement and mental health agencies on topics of crisis intervention and suicidology. He is a licensed psychologist and is listed in the *National Register of Health Service Providers in Psychology.*